Cynthia Newberry

Adrian Daub
What Tech Calls Thinking

Adrian Daub is a professor of comparative literature and
German studies at Stanford University and the director
of Stanford's Michelle R. Clayman Institute for Gender
Research, and he is the author of several books. His research focuses on the intersection of literature, music,
and philosophy in the nineteenth century. His writing
has appeared in *The Guardian*, *The New Republic*, *n+1*,
Longreads, and the *Los Angeles Review of Books*. He lives
in San Francisco.

What Tech Calls Thinking

FSG Originals × *Logic*

FARRAR, STRAUS AND GIROUX

New York

What
Tech
Calls
Thinking

■ ■ ■

An Inquiry into the Intellectual Bedrock
of Silicon Valley

■

Adrian Daub

FSG Originals × *Logic*
Farrar, Straus and Giroux
120 Broadway, New York 10271

Printed in the United States of America
First edition, 2020

Library of Congress Cataloging-in-Publication Data
Names: Daub, Adrian, author.
Title: What tech calls thinking / Adrian Daub.
Description: First edition. | New York : FSG Originals, Farrar, Straus
    and Giroux, 2020. | Series: FSG Originals × *Logic*
Identifiers: LCCN 2020013401 | ISBN 9780374538644 (paperback)
Subjects: LCSH: Internet industry—California, Northern. | High
    technology industries—California, Northern. | Technology—Social
    aspects—California, Northern. | Information technology—History. |
    Technological innovations—History.
Classification: LCC HD9696.8.U63 C343 2020 | DDC 338.4/
    7609794—dc23
LC record available at https://lccn.loc.gov/2020013401

Our books may be purchased in bulk for promotional,
educational, or business use. Please contact your local bookseller
or the Macmillan Corporate and Premium Sales Department at
1-800-221-7945, extension 5442, or by e-mail at
MacmillanSpecialMarkets@macmillan.com.

www.fsgoriginals.com • www.fsgbooks.com • www.logicmag.io
Follow us on Twitter, Facebook, and Instagram at @fsgoriginals and
@logic_magazine

10 9 8 7 6 5 4 3 2 1

Contents

■ ■ ■

What Tech Calls Thinking

Introduction

This is a book about the history of ideas in a place that likes to pretend its ideas don't have any history. The tech industry is largely disinterested in the kinds of questions this book raises; tech companies simply create a product and then look to market it. Mark Zuckerberg put it as follows: "I hadn't been very good about communicating that we were trying to go for this mission. We just showed up every day and kind of did what we thought was the right next thing to do." The mission, the big question, became important only later. Only in hindsight did he have to ask himself: How do I explain this to journalists? The U.S. House of Representatives? Myself? At the same time, Zuckerberg's quote is meant to imply that there *had* been such a mission all along, that showing up every day and working on a good, monetizable product was never all Facebook was about. *What Tech Calls Thinking* concerns where tech entrepreneurs and the press outlets that adore them look once they reach the point at which they need to contextualize what they're doing—when their narrative has to fit into a broader story about the world in which we all live and work.

As Silicon Valley reshapes the world, journalists, academics, and activists are spending more time scrutinizing the high-minded ideals by which companies like Google and Facebook claim to be guided. As the journalist Franklin Foer put it, Silicon Valley companies "have a set of ideals, but they also have a business model. They end up reconfiguring your ideals in order to justify their business model." This book asks where companies' ideals come from. The question is far from a sideshow: It concerns how the changes Silicon Valley brings about are made plausible and made to seem inevitable. It concerns the way those involved in the tech industry understand their projects and the industry's relationship to the wider world. It isn't so much about the words that people in Silicon Valley use to describe their day-to-day business— interesting books could be and have been written about the thinking contained in terms like "user," "platform," or "design." Rather, it is about what the tech world thinks it's doing when it looks beyond its day-to-day business—the part about changing the world, about disrupting X or liberating Y. The stuff about Tahrir Square protests and $27 donations. What ideas begin to track then? And what is their provenance?

Indeed, the very fact that these ideas *have* histories matters. Silicon Valley is good at "reframing" questions, problems, and solutions, as the jargon of "design thinking" puts it. And it is often deeply unclear what the relationship is between the "reframed" versions and the original ones. It's easy to come away with the sense that the original way of stating the problem is made irrelevant by the reframing. That perhaps even the original problem is made irrelevant. Some of this is probably inherent in technological change: it's hard to remember the history of something that changes how memory works, after all. In the 1960s, the communication theorist Marshall McLuhan (1911–1980) proposed that "the effects of technology do not occur at the level of opinions or concepts, but alter sense ratios or patterns of perception steadily and without any resistance."

But clearly that's only part of the story. To some extent, the amnesia around the concepts that tech companies draw on to make public policy (without admitting that they are doing so) is by design. Fetishizing the novelty of the problem (or at least its "framing") deprives the public of the analytic tools it has previously brought to bear on similar problems. Granted, quite frequently these technologies are truly novel—but the companies that pioneer them use that novelty to suggest that traditional categories of understanding don't do them justice, when in fact standard analytic tools largely apply just fine. But this practice tends to disenfranchise all of the people with a long tradition of analyzing these problems—whether they're experts, activists, academics, union organizers, journalists, or politicians.

Consider how much mileage the tech industry has gotten out of its technological determinism. The industry likes to imbue the changes it yields with the character of natural law: If I or my team don't do this, someone else will. Such determinism influences how students pick what companies to work for; it influences what work they're willing to do there. Or consider how important words like "disruption" and "innovation" are to the sway the tech industry holds over our collective imagination. How they sweep aside certain parts of the status quo but leave other parts mysteriously untouched. How they implicitly cast you as a stick-in-the-mud if you ask how much revolution someone is capable of when that person represents billions in venture capital investment.

This is where the limits of our thinking very quickly

become the limits of our politics. What if what goes by the name of innovation is ultimately just an opportunistic exploitation of regulatory gaps? And before we blame those gaps, keep in mind that regulation is supposed to be slow-moving, deliberate, a little bit after-the-fact. A lot of tech companies make their home between the moment some new way to make money is discovered and the moment some government entity gets around to deciding if it's actually legal. In fact, they frequently plonk down their headquarters there.

Take Uber and Lyft, for example. The two ride-share giants are in many ways more agile and cheaper for the consumer than the taxi services they're slowly destroying, and these companies are accordingly popular with large investment funds, for one primary reason: their drivers are independent contractors who have no bargaining power, no benefits, and very few legal protections. Everything these companies do—from the rewards programs they set up for their contractors to the way the algorithms that assign rides to drivers seem to punish casual driving—is actually designed to nudge their drivers inch by inch toward a full-time employment that they aren't allowed to call full-time employment. The moment this state of affairs is recognized, all kinds of rules will apply to these companies, making them even more unprofitable and likely putting them out of business. But until such a moment, the companies will explain to you ad nauseam how they're different and new and how you are missing the point when you apply established categories to them.

This book is about concepts and ideas that pretend to be novel but that are actually old motifs playing dress-up in a hoodie. The rhetoric of Silicon Valley may seem un-precedented, but in truth it is steeped in some pretty long-standing American traditions—from the tent revival to the infomercial, from predestination to self-help. The point of concepts in general is to help us make distinctions that matter, but the concepts I discuss in the chapters that follow frequently serve to obscure such distinctions. The inverse can also be true: some of the concepts in this book aim to create distinctions where there are none. Again and again we'll come across two phenomena that to the untrained eye look identical, but a whole propaganda industry exists to tell us they are not. Taxi company loses money; Uber loses money—apparently not the same. The tech industry ideas portrayed in this book are not wrong, but they allow the rich and powerful to make distinctions without difference, and elide differences that are politically important to recognize. They aren't dangerous ideas in themselves. Their danger lies in the fact that they will probably lead to bad thinking.

In the following chapters, I will try to show not only how certain ideas permeate the world of the tech industry, but also how that industry represents itself to a press hungry for tech heroes and villains, for spectacular stories in what is ultimately a pretty unspectacular industry. A study like this one almost by necessity has to foreground the highly visible founders, funders, and thought leaders. To find out how ordinary coders or designers think, to say nothing of all the folks making up the tech industry who aren't customarily thought of as belonging to that industry, is a very interesting project in its own right, but it isn't the project of this book. For better and for worse, the media has a fixation on tech *thought* leaders. It seems to need certain figures to be able to spin its narrative. Peter Thiel, Elon Musk, Steve Jobs, and others like them knew how to manipulate that—something they learned from another California global export: 1960s counterculture.

Unfortunately, my own spotlighting of these leaders means this book risks recapitulating one of the central misperceptions of the tech industry; it's anything but clear whether figures like Mark Zuckerberg, Elon Musk, or even Steve Jobs really embody the way the tech sector understands itself. But what is clear is that they represent the way the tech sector has communicated with the outside world. They are easy identificatory figures when one is dealing with an industry that can be disturbingly amorphous and decentralized. (This is, after all, how the *pars pro toto* "Silicon Valley" has functioned in general.) They are creatures of the media, inviting us to project our fears, giving shape to our hopes. Most important, they encourage us to think that someone, whether charismatic or nefarious, knows where the journey is going. Visibility in the press is not, of course, the same as representativeness. Making a Theranos movie is not cool. You know what's cool? Making an Elizabeth Holmes movie.

Giving these ideas' history back is central to any attempt to interrogate the claims the tech industry makes about itself. But there's another question that we can ask once we've figured out where these ideas come from: Why were these ideas convenient to adapt, and why was it convenient to forget their history? The story of these ideas intersects with the great transformations that information technology has undergone in the last seventy years. Coding went from being clerical busywork done by women to a well-paid profession dominated by men. In recent years, competencies around technology went from highly specialized to broadly distributed, to the point where "learn to code" has become a panacea for any and all of the ravages of capitalism.

And the environment around tech has changed: the government went from basically owning the tech industry to struggling to regulate it; computer science went from an exotic field seeking to establish itself to one of the most popular university majors. The cultural visibility of the sector and its practices has transformed even since the film *The Social Network* came out in 2010. Perhaps Foer had it only half right: When the companies of Silicon Valley reconfigure your ideals, it's not just in order to sustain their business model. It's also to avoid cognitive dissonance in their thinking about gender, race, class, history, and capitalism.

Many of the ideas traced in this book had analogous trajectories. For one thing, they emerged from a similar era. They were new ideas when given definitive shape in the sixties, frequently by the counterculture. They attained their shape outside of the university, though they were always on the periphery of it. As the management-science scholar Stephen Adams has pointed out, a lot of the institutions of learning and research featured in this book grew out of a desire to stanch a persistent brain drain of bright young people moving from the West Coast eastward. Around these institutions sprang up a network of highly educated but also highly idiosyncratic thinkers bent on shaking up the system. They were the ones who injected these ideas into the emerging discourses around a burgeoning industry.

The early fate of these ideas was bound up with institutions that had little to do with commerce: from research centers to hippie retreats, from universities to communes. The fact that the people interested in these ideas made a lot of money was almost beside the point: they founded companies because they thought of them as spontaneous, communal correctives to the overly stolid institutions of government and the university. But before long, shibboleths like "communication" and "big data" circulated less and less because of their cultural cachet and more and more because of the vagaries of the business cycle. What hasn't changed: formal education seeming secondary to these ideas—but where previously that had meant dropping out to pursue niche projects, it soon came to mean dropping out to make lots of money. The ideas that tech calls thinking were developed and refined in the making of money.

And what tech calls thinking may be undergoing a further shift. Fred Turner, a professor of communication at Stanford, traced the intellectual origins of Silicon Valley in his book *From Counterculture to Cyberculture* (2006). The generation Turner covered in that book came of age in the sixties, and if they made money in the Valley, they're playing tennis in Woodside now; if they taught, they are mostly retiring. The ethos is changing. "As little as ten years ago," Turner told me, "the look for a programmer was still long hair, potbelly, Gryffindor T-shirt. I don't see that as much anymore."

The generation of thinkers and innovators Turner wrote about still read entire books of philosophy; they had Ph.D.s; they had gotten interested in computers because computers allowed them to ask big questions that previously had been impossible to ask, let alone answer. Eric Roberts is of that generation. He got his Ph.D. in 1980 and taught at Wellesley before coming to Stanford. He shaped into the form they take today two of the courses that together are the gateway to Stanford's computer science major. CS 106A, Programming Methodologies, and 106B, Programming Abstractions, are a rite of passage for Stanford students; almost all students, whether they are computer science majors or not, enroll in one or the other during their time at the university. Roberts's other course was CS 181, Computers, Ethics, and Public Policy. Back in the day, CS 181 was a small writing class that prepared computer scientists for the ethical ramifications of their inventions. Today it is a massive class, capped at a hundred students, that has become one more thing hundreds of majors check off their lists before they graduate. Eric Roberts left Stanford in 2015, and today teaches much smaller classes at Reed College in Portland.

As Roberts tells it, the real change happened in 2008, though "it almost happened in the eighties, it almost happened in the nineties." During those tech booms, the number of computer science majors exploded, to the point where the faculty had trouble teaching enough classes for them. "But then," Roberts says, "the dot-com bust probably saved us." The number of majors declined precipitously when after the bubble burst media reports were full of laid-off dot-com employees. Most of those employees were back to making good money again by 2002, but the myth of precariousness persisted—until the Great Recession, that is, which was when what Roberts calls the "get-rich-quick crowd" was forced out of investment banking and started looking back at the ship they had prematurely jumped from in 2001. When venture capital got burned in the real estate market and in finance after 2008, for instance, it came west, ready to latch on to something new. The tech industry we know today is what happens when certain received notions meet with a massive amount of cash with nowhere else to go.

⁚⁚

David M. Kelley, a Stanford professor and the founder of the design company IDEO, is one of the apostles behind design thinking. He has shaped the way Silicon Valley has presented and marketed itself since at least the 1980s. He is a founder of the Hasso Plattner Institute of Design at Stanford, also known as the "d.school," and has been a fixture at TED Talks and developers' conferences. In one TED Talk back in 2002, Kelley gave a series of examples of how design thinking was changing the tech industry—and an inadvertent example of what tech calls thinking. For a long time, Kelley told his audience, tech companies were "focused on products or objects." But in recent years, "we've kind of climbed Maslow's hierarchy a little bit," focusing more on "human-centeredness" in design.

But why mention Maslow's hierarchy? Maslow's famous model tried to explain how certain human needs can emerge and be satisfied only after other, more fundamental needs are met. The idea Kelley is describing, by contrast, is indeed one that many philosophers—the entire school of phenomenology, for one—have wrestled with. But Maslow, specifically, did not. In context, all Kelley seems to be saying is that designers used to think about objects in one way, and now they have begun thinking about them in another, more complex way, because they now design "behaviors and personality into products." They have recognized that how people relate to objects is more complicated than they once supposed. So far, so good. But why invoke the psychologist Abraham Maslow (1908–1970) to make that point?

This is where we start getting a sense for what tech calls thinking. Kelley doesn't say, "The philosopher Martin Heidegger proposed that human subjectivity can be understood only as a mode of being-in-the-world," or anything like that. He does not go for a piece of philosophy that is apropos but that might alienate the audience at a TED Talk. He adduces a bit of pop psychology that has become a kind of byword since Maslow came up with it in 1943. And the way he brings Maslow up seems to matter too: Kelley doesn't stop to cite or to explain in detail; a quick, ornamental wave of the hand is enough. Many of the ideas in this book function like this—they are held in common, broadly shared and easily pointed to, even if no one takes the time to figure out where they come from or whether they are correctly applied. Many ideas like this are held by people who don't actually subscribe to the philosophy from which they come—or do subscribe to it and don't realize it.

Another thing made Maslow's hierarchy a convenient shorthand in a TED Talk: it's an idea with strong regional ties. Maslow spent some of the last years of his life in California. He became important at Esalen, the New Age retreat along the Pacific Coast Highway; he worked for a private foundation in Menlo Park, just up El Camino Real from Stanford. One thing that surprised me in writing this book is just how local these kinds of ideas are. There are thinkers in this book who, had they not relocated to the Bay Area, or, in the case of Maslow, literally pulled into the driveway of the Esalen Institute, surely wouldn't be looming nearly as large in the reservoir of tech's received ideas. There may be some local pride at work in Kelley's mentioning Maslow. There may be a sense of genealogy, a line of tradition being drawn from New Age psychotherapy and leftist intentional communities to the TED Talk.

Still, the localism is pretty remarkable, given that one of the great achievements of this industry has been to open up the world in hitherto-unimaginable ways. But it is a local story. The tech industry recruits from specific milieus, nations, schools, social classes, and so forth. The age spread, especially at the smaller and fast-growing companies, can be extremely limited, and many of the older figures these companies interact with (the venture capitalists and lawyers, for example) are basically them five years older. Silicon Valley loves the words "everyone," "universal," and "people," but what they usually mean is "people I went to school with," "my housemates in East Palo Alto," or "my four immediate subordinates." The universality that their business model pushes them toward exists in tension with the fact that they actually know very few people.

It's also characteristic that, even though he teaches at Stanford, Kelley didn't invoke a university professor. Maslow was an academic, but he worked at a private research institution in the Valley. What tech calls thinking is done largely outside, but within shouting distance of, the university. One of the more famous protagonists of tech's love-hate relationship to academia is Peter Thiel, who made a fortune by working at PayPal and investing in companies like Facebook, and who is famously wary of higher education. The Thiel Fellowships pay young people not to go to college, and Thiel publicly asserts that he thinks the university is a bubble—but he nevertheless spent almost a decade at Stanford, where he received both a bachelor's degree and a law degree, and, when he visits, is a welcome presence at the Faculty Club. Elon Musk likes to portray himself as having an autodidact's mind, and, indeed, he dropped out of a Ph.D. program at Stanford—but he too spent a lot of time at universities, in both Canada and the United States. The ideas in this book are university-adjacent, academish. They cannot free themselves of the institution any more than they can be made fully at home there. And the mode by which they are best acquired is the subject of the first chapter: dropping out.

.1.

Dropping Out

In the fall of 2007, Denise Winters was working at the registrar's office at Stanford University as a student services officer. One of her duties was handling forms that students filled out in order to take a leave of absence from the university. The forms asked students to provide some information as to why they were seeking to take time off from college. Most of them wrote about sick relatives, medical problems, feeling overwhelmed. "Don't write a novel," she'd tell them. "In the end, it's your business." Still, even by that standard, the reason given by one student that fall was unusually terse. "What's a 23andMe?" she remembers asking.

No one knows exactly how many Stanford students have left the university to join or start companies in information technology or biotech without attaining their degrees. The university doesn't collect data on reasons students leave, which itself is a holdover from a time when dropping out was a blot on your CV, not something you trumpeted all over CNBC. Stanford administrators say the numbers are probably higher than at other universities of Stanford's caliber, but they're not huge. Still, that fairly contained number of dropouts has had an outsize purchase on the way the public imagines the tech industry and the whiz kids who have shaped its most recent iteration. You weave one sort of legend when you say you are "Harvard educated," but there's a certain other kind of legend you weave only if you can say that you dropped out of Harvard.

Elizabeth Holmes, the former CEO of the biotech startup Theranos, who is currently on trial for wire fraud and conspiracy in a San Jose court, seems to have understood that better than anyone. SHE'S AMERICA'S YOUNGEST FEMALE BILLIONAIRE, a CNN headline declared in October 2014, AND A DROPOUT. Almost every fawning profile published over the years mentioned the fact that Holmes had dropped out of Stanford, perhaps more religiously than they would have mentioned Stanford if she'd actually graduated. It felt like another item on her CV. And almost every article referenced a rogues' gallery of famous prior dropouts (whose memories Holmes certainly meant to invoke when she decided to leave the Farm prematurely): Bill Gates, Steve Jobs, Mark Zuckerberg.

In fact, Holmes had left Stanford a little more than ten years before the CNN headline, and raised a million dollars from her former neighbor in Los Altos Hills, Tim Draper, who just happened to be one of Silicon Valley's most well-regarded venture capitalists. Oh, and some money from her Stanford friend's dad, who ran a medical device company in Taiwan. Oh, and some from her family. Calling Holmes a "dropout" was both accurate and an object lesson in how two actions can resemble each other but mean completely different things. There's an interesting dual consciousness at work when investors, the press, and the public fawn over dropouts like these but also worry about a "dropout epidemic" among very different kinds of kids. Somewhat hilariously, much of the recent hand-wringing about a "dropout epidemic" came about due to a report by the Gates Foundation. But that cognitive dissonance is probably the point: don't do what Bill Gates did, kids, unless you're Bill Gates.

Dropping out of an elite university to start a company means tapping into a narrative. It's a nice way of associating with a prestigious place while also not really associating with it. It's elitism that very visibly snubs the elite; or, perhaps even better, snubbing the elite while nevertheless basking in its glow. But it's worth asking: What kind of an education is dropping out? Because the quintessential tech wunderkind as portrayed by the media noticeably doesn't *not* go to college. He or she goes to college in a new way—by showing up, taking a few classes, making a few friends, and then dropping out. As we shall see, in Silicon Valley in particular, the act of dropping out conjures a set of associations that have more to do with sixties counterculture than with entrepreneurial success, but which share with the famous tech dropouts a vocabulary of unconventional thinking and independence.

It also creates a challenge for historians who want to show what influences shape the current crop of founders. There have been professors at Stanford who taught nearly every technologist who graduated from the institution, so it's safe to assume that some aspect of how they have thought about computers has influenced their former students. The founders of Google credit Terry Winograd with shaping the way their famous venture turned out. How does this equation change when the encounter with academic thought is less about getting trained and more about a momentary, utilitarian flyby? When the university is less about patient incubation of talent than a brief pollination with prestige and some cool ideas?

This chapter provides the basis for all the terms explored in the following chapters. How do concepts like communication or content function when the person using them has encountered their extremely long and rich histories in the context of a general ed course, talked them over with roommates, and then left the university to figure out how to make credit card payments easier? How do these concepts work when you've basically gotten the gist, but perhaps not much more than the gist?

Anyone who's gone to college in the United States knows that it can be a scattered experience: random requirements, exciting but seemingly disparate course offerings, choices determined by time conflicts and departmental whims. This is particularly true the first few years—that is, the only ones a dropout typically spends at school. No one seems to have gone to the trouble of finding out what courses Mark Zuckerberg took at Harvard before he dropped out in 2004. What gets noted is CS 121 with Professor Harry Lewis (partly because Bill Gates took it as well before he jumped ship) and his major in psychology (presumably because Facebook plays with our psychology, even though Zuckerberg himself has said that he hadn't taken many classes in the field by the time he left). He mentioned taking the introductory economics course EC 10 in his 2017 commencement speech there.

So even though Zuckerberg almost certainly would have taken courses from Harvard's core curriculum (in eleven areas, such as "moral reasoning" and "foreign cultures"), the courses that have made it into popular legend are the ones that seem predictive of what he would do after he left Harvard early. The funny thing is, that's not really how college works for most people. Every year I get emails from anguished parents asking me what their kid could possibly do with a degree in, say, feminist, gender, and sexuality studies—and I answer, pretty much anything. Somehow the act of dropping out changes that equation: the liberal arts aspect of the American college experience drops out too. College becomes predictive and vocational in a way that (four-year) college really isn't supposed to be, especially at the places people drop out of and are then commended for having dropped out of.

Mark Zuckerberg is on record saying, "I probably learned more coding from random side projects that I did than the courses I took in college." The dropout's relationship to college is pretty openly transactional. The idea of a holistic education, of the liberal arts, of the well-rounded student, of the future responsible citizen all depend on you going through a curated educational program. Cynics might say that's why colleges are so happy to promote these ideas, given that they entail your handing over four years' worth of cash to them. But that isn't how the dropouts see it. They simply approach college as customers, and vaguely dissatisfied ones at that. With the exception of Peter Thiel, who seems locked in some weird I-don't-know-whether-to-kiss-you-or-kill-you codependency with higher education, most dropouts appear to look at college as a sort of forgettable experience. But that requires shifting what you consider part of college.

When CNBC reported Zuckerberg's remarks, it framed them as his saying he "learned more from a hobby than he did at Harvard." But that's not quite what Zuckerberg said. He said he learned more *coding* from a hobby than he did in his Harvard *courses*. And he had these hobbies while enrolled at Harvard; one would probably say they were part of his Harvard experience. Moreover, the metonymy "Harvard" is not identical to the courses you take there—and no one would likely agree more with the idea that you can learn just as much "from random side projects" than the universities themselves, which, after all, market their incredibly expensive dorm accommodations using the same justification. Not for nothing did Zuckerberg take most of Facebook's other founders from Harvard. But CNBC wanted to frame Zuckerberg's remarks as a rejection of the university. In the dominant discourse about dropping out, several things are equated that in our own lives we know to be unequal: university equals the courses you took; the courses you took equal the courses that prepared you for eventual business success.

To be clear: Zuckerberg wasn't advising that you drop out of college when he brought up his Harvard side projects. He gave the example to illustrate the importance of being creative "outside of the jobs you've done." So, once again, CNBC's framing is off, but at the same time, Zuckerberg is perhaps revealing how he thought of college: It was his first job. He stuck it out long enough to learn what he needed to learn, but when it turned stale and a new opportunity came along, he hopped firms. Anyone who's watched people switch jobs in tech, especially in Silicon Valley, has seen this habit in action: there is a genuine fear among young and talented tech workers in Silicon Valley of staying too long at a company whose luster has dimmed, whose tech no longer gets anyone excited. There's the panic in people's eyes as they admit to being at the same startup that still, even after two or three years, no one has heard of and no one cares about.

Elizabeth Holmes arrived at Stanford in September 2002; she dropped out in the winter quarter of 2004. I should be clear that I did not view her transcripts; doing that would have been creepy and probably illegal. But I have advised enough students at Stanford to surmise what her brief brush with the university would have looked like. She would have been required to take what was then known as the Introduction to the Humanities program, a general education requirement intended to "build an intellectual foundation in the study of human thought, values, beliefs, creativity, and culture." In the fall of 2002, this would have meant taking a big-picture class like Visions of Mortality, or Citizenship, or Thinking with Nature—there were eight different ones on offer that quarter—and a sequence of two more specific courses in the winter and spring quarters of 2003. In practice, the fall courses were structured around five great books spanning much of recorded history (start with Gilgamesh, end with a comic book); the winter and spring courses were designed around a set of ten great books drawn from a narrower orbit.

Holmes would also have taken a course in the Program in Writing and Rhetoric (PWR, pronounced "power"), a two-quarter sequence unless she'd gotten a 4 or 5 on her English AP, in which case an accelerated one-quarter version was available. There was a language requirement, though it's possible the Mandarin-immersion classes she took in high school allowed her to place out of it. In her first quarter at Stanford, the journalist John Carreyrou reports, she took an introductory seminar, most likely one called Drug Delivery in the 21st Century, with Channing Robertson, who would eventually go on to help Theranos get initial funding. She also seems to have taken Robertson's Introduction to Chemical Engineering in the spring quarter—and then, it seems, she was gone.

The reason I'm dwelling on this Stanford inside baseball is to point out that the kind of preparation conjured up by the phrase "a Stanford dropout" is in fact the exact opposite of what her preparation looked like. In a 2009 interview, Holmes said—and the irony should take your breath away in hindsight—that she decided that "another few classes in chemical engineering was not necessary" for what she had in mind. In another interview she said, "I was trained as an engineer." When she said these things, back before her massive fraud became apparent, it must have been easy to nod along and think, Yes, it's true, one *can* probably learn a lot during one magical, pressurized year of intensive study in a place brimming with like-minded, motivated young people. Perhaps in such a setting it is possible to pick up all the skills one needs. But the fact is, that's not the education Holmes received. It's the education she would have received—after working on her Writing and Rhetoric, getting her general education requirements out of the way, brushing up on her Mandarin, and exploring some Visions of Mortality or something along those lines.

A lot of professors worry about dropouts because they see them as part of an assault on "liberal education": the dropout, they think, treats the university as a vocational school and totally ignores its attempts to shape well-rounded individuals and good citizens. And maybe that indeed is what a dropout does. But ironically, it turns out that in nearly all U.S. institutions, the dropout gets *only* the general stuff. Does that affect the way someone thinks? If so, it might not mean that dropouts leave as narrow thinkers. Holmes would have (probably) read her way through twenty-five books of the Western canon, which is sort of respectable, while her preparation for running a biotech startup consisted of—and I'm quoting from the course description here—"guest scientists and engineers describ[ing] products on the market and in the pipeline," as well as "field trips."

Dropouts risk leaving as thinkers for whom there are perfectly true but relatively shallow generalities on the one hand, and myopic problems on the other. The vast gulf between the two is what the later years of their college experience would have filled in. That's when these big-picture questions come to bear on rather fiddly issues unique to a certain field. At Stanford, unfortunately, the later years are also when most engineers take their ethics requirement. Who knows where Elizabeth Holmes would be today if they had front-loaded it back in 2002?

※

But when dropouts like Elizabeth Holmes deliberately invoke earlier successful tech dropouts as they pack up their dorm rooms, they also tap into a much longer history of dropping out—one that they may be less aware of.

Origin stories are ubiquitous in Silicon Valley. Companies have them, founders have them, even random employees seem to engage in mythmaking. Such stories are probably necessary because the products made in Silicon Valley, and the places where the magic happens, are not that spectacular to look at—but investors, journalists, and the public nonetheless need something to gawk at. Society is fascinated by the dropout because most people, almost by definition, did not drop out. Fetishizing the break allows journalists and the public to turn a couple of fairly random, and frequently predictable, decisions into a coherent narrative. But in a strange way, maybe it has the same function for some of tech's protagonists too. In an industry that idealizes independence but relies (as most industries do) on by-now-well-established pipelines, there must be considerable cognitive dissonance between how you're asked to present yourself and how you really are. You're encouraged to present as risk-taking what was really just adherence to rules, as eccentricity what was actually widely shared common wisdom, and as a late triumph after incredible adversity what was in fact basically inevitable.

It is in this context that dropping out of college became the shiny, distracting object it is today. The founders themselves are much less likely to bring it up, relying on others to do it for them. And those others always do. You can almost hear desperate journalists seizing on the minor biographical variances of upper-middle-class white youth in order to be able to say *something* about these people. In their narratives, line-jumping of any kind becomes the mark of genius. When Elizabeth Holmes was still on the cover of *Fortune*, profiles of her would make much of the fact that as a first-year she talked her way into a lab *with Ph.D. students*. (How many labs *without* Ph.D. students are you aware of, and should we maybe shut them down?) Having taught oneself to code in high school is a staple. Holmes's knowledge of Mandarin (she took summer school classes) was another detail trotted out with a feeling that surely somehow it *had* to be significant and interesting. All these things are perfectly ordinary, and no two people move through their collegiate experience in the same manner. Somehow the sudden heights of success to which these young people climb make people fixate on biographical data points that are, upon reflection, absolutely unremarkable.

It's probably not an accident that people who begin and then ostentatiously reject an elite education more often than not eventually find themselves in the San Francisco Bay Area, a place where the phrase "dropping out" carries certain historic echoes, connotes certain unfulfilled promises, that are both related and entirely different. "Turn on, tune in, drop out" is the famous mantra Timothy Leary made popular at the Human Be-In in Golden Gate Park in 1967. It's worth keeping this sense of dropping out in mind when one considers the mythology of famous tech industry college dropouts.

Like our modern dropouts, Leary frequently linked dropping out to mythmaking: "To drop out, you must form your own religion." Sure, it might put you in touch with some preexisting energy, the "ancient heavenly connection to the starry dynamo in the machinery of night," as Allen Ginsberg put it. But to some extent you were supposed to invent the connection, Leary thought: "You select a myth as a reminder that you are part of an ancient and holy process. You select a myth to guide you when you drop out of the narrow confines of the fake-prop studio set." Selecting a myth is a key idea here: you give up a certain amount of control when you drop out, but you retain control over the meaning of what's happening to you. Dropping out is at once a return into the self and an opening toward the world.

In Hermann Hesse's novel *Steppenwolf*, which had been published in 1927 but came back into fashion with the beatniks, the saxophonist Pablo, who lures the main character, Harry Haller, into a mind-expanding magic theater, speaks of another world that exists "only within yourself." He hands Harry a looking glass through which the latter sees "the reflection of an uneasy self-tormented, inwardly laboring and seething being—myself, Harry Haller. And within him again I saw the Steppenwolf, a shy, beautiful, dazed wolf with frightened eyes that smoldered now with anger, now with sadness." Dropping out severs you from the "robot performances on the TV-studio stage," as Leary put it. It instead orients you toward your inner Steppenwolf.

Aldous Huxley thought acid put you in touch with "the antipodes," areas of your mind that are eclipsed in normal functioning. But in Harry Haller's case, withdrawing into your own individuality is about casting off parts of the self that are constructed or deformed by outside forces, by societal expectations, and above all by educational institutions. Hesse had had a miserable time in school, and many of the countercultural thinkers who rediscovered him in the 1950s and '60s, from Jack Kerouac to Ken Kesey, similarly hated the conventions of thought and living that were imposed by formal schooling. This is what Chief Bromden in *One Flew Over the Cuckoo's Nest* (1962) calls simply "the nation-wide Combine that's the really big force." So even though Leary's sense of dropping out wasn't explicitly about school, the consonance isn't an accident either.

It is central to the idea of dropping out that by withdrawing into your own particular self, you actually get tuned in to a broader, more global consciousness. This was what the counterculture had over those earlier texts that are more resigned in their rebellion. Rejecting the Combine, rejecting conventional authority, will not drive you insane the way it does Chief Bromden, will not isolate you the way it does Harry Haller, and will not ruin you the way it does McMurphy, the *Cuckoo's Nest* protagonist. Instead, it puts you in touch with others who are similarly disenchanted. In fact, rejection alone allows you to see the world without the blind spots conventional thinking and morality impose on our seeing.

In Robert Heinlein's 1961 novel, *Stranger in a Strange Land*, the Martians give this the name "grokking," a mode of understanding that is individual and collective at once: it means, we are told, "to merge, blend, intermarry, lose identity in group experience. It means almost everything that we mean by religion, philosophy, and science—and,"

Heinlein's novel adds, "it means as little to us," meaning earthbound humans, "as color means to a blind man." This too is part of grokking: in order for you to get it, everyone else must not get it. The word "grok" quickly made it into the counterculture's vocabulary, showing up in the work of Ram Dass (whose 1971 *Be Here Now* Steve Jobs cited as an early inspiration) and in Tom Wolfe's firsthand description of the sixties counterculture, *The Electric Kool-Aid Acid Test* (1968), although Wolfe misuses it. But before long it made its way into the parlance of computer culture.

There are serious disagreements among these books about what exactly you transcend when you drop out. But there is perhaps a more obvious, and therefore less noticed, disagreement on *when* you transcend. Although Harry Haller's age is never stated in *Steppenwolf*, he is clearly middle-aged. He is well established in the society he rejects. Will Farnaby, who discovers a utopian Polynesian society in Aldous Huxley's *Island* (1962), is a disillusioned middle manager. And while Kerouac is a quintessential young person's writer, Sal Paradise starts the road trip in *On the Road* (1957) to get over a divorce.

When it appropriated these heroes, the counterculture of the sixties aged them down quite a bit. Suddenly, you didn't have to experience work life, family life, and adult life to grow disillusioned with it. You could be disillusioned even before you joined the machine. But in tech this wasn't really true—the evangelists of what Turner calls the "cybernetic counterculture," such as the artists and theorists of USCO ("Us Company"), were in their thirties by the late sixties. Their idols, including Marshall McLuhan and R. Buckminster Fuller, were even older.

Meaning they had a good sense of the world they were rebelling against. So did Leary (forty-six when he addressed the Human Be-In) and Kesey (thirty when he threw the first Acid Test). The average college dropout is significantly younger, and their vision quest is for that reason quite different. That's not to discount their vision, but rather to say that their sense of the society that vision opposes isn't that likely to be as developed.

Professors at Stanford see students drop out with some regularity. Stanford's previous president even invested in a couple of ventures undertaken by students who had dropped out to pursue them, which raised some eyebrows. Call it a kind of for-profit Thiel Fellowship. When students do drop out, it's spoken of in hushed tones, the way you'd comment on someone's placing a giant bet at a roulette table. These kids must have something *really* special, to wager their futures like this. You almost get the sense that this mythos is sort of the point—that without the sense of urgency, risk, and free fall created by the act of dropping out, maybe the startup idea wouldn't seem as exciting to investors and journalists.

While being careful not to talk about individual students, I will point out that the atmosphere of risk appears to be massively overstated. Mark Zuckerberg admitted he knew "I'd be fine if Facebook didn't work out." And while at Stanford we rarely see those dropouts who go on to make boatloads of money again, in my experience, those whose startups either go bust or don't do as well as the dropouts hoped eventually come back and get their degrees. They're not crawling back either; it's evidently almost as well traveled a road as the one leading prematurely out of Stanford and into the incubators of Mountain View and Redwood City. So perhaps it's better to think of dropping out as the ultimate semester-abroad experience. You're leaving college, but are you really *leaving* college?

And for all the echoes of the anti-authoritarian sixties, the break with the collegiate environment is far from a rejection, especially when it comes to social aspects. Zuckerberg dropped out of Harvard and quickly moved into what sounds like a frat house in Palo Alto. In several massive Victorians around Alamo Square Park in San Francisco, you can find communal live-work spaces that resemble a mix of the fanciest hippie commune you've ever seen with the fanciest dormitory you can imagine. This in spite of the fact that its denizens are about as far from collegiate age as Zuckerberg is now.

And, as in the case of Zuckerberg's venture, the business models of so many of these startups carry some aspect of the collegiate experience into the wider culture. "The Facebook" started out as an online equivalent of a service that college students had long taken for granted and relied on for dating, judging, and stalking—an actual, physical, lowercase "facebook." Now everybody could get in on the fun. The famous knock against tech startups is that about 90 percent of them seem aimed at answering the question, "What things isn't my mom doing for me anymore?" But probably the question should read, "What will I do now that I no longer have access to a dining hall, a laundry service, a ready-made dating pool, or a student directory?"

Tinder frames itself as the high-tech equivalent of a frat party. It seems that by turning their back on college, the dropouts make the outside world look and behave a little more like the groves of academe.

These are extreme examples, of course, but they set the tone for the entire industry. Tech professionalizes early, but professionalizes less. You draw a regular salary and know what you're doing with your life earlier than your peers, but you subsist on Snickers and Soylent far longer. You are prematurely self-directed and at the same time infantilized in ways that resemble college life for much longer than almost anyone in your age cohort. Eric Roberts, who has taught generations of aspiring tech workers at Stanford, has observed that some of his less enthusiastic students choose tech not out of a desire for money but rather out of a desire to stay near campus: "Just wanting to stay in Santa Clara County militates for taking a job at a tech company," he points out.

All of this seems to define the way tech practices dropping out of college: It's a gesture of risk-taking that's actually largely drained of risk. It's a gesture of rejection that seems stuck on the very thing it's supposedly rejecting.

Dropping out is still understood as a rejection of a certain elite. But it is an anti-elitism whose very point is to usher you as quickly as possible into another elite— the elite of those who are sufficiently tuned in, the elite of those who get it, the ones who see through the world that the squares are happy to inhabit. This was as true for Leary and his cohort as it is for Zuckerberg and his. Dropping out may feel like you're opening yourself up to a wider world, but in most cases you just shut yourself off from the world in a new way. This has shaped a certain kind of discourse—witness how Donald Trump has leveraged anti-elitism while being convinced that you need a picture ID to buy a head of lettuce.

It has certainly shaped the tech industry's somewhat tortured relationship to universality. The tech giants want to make things happen for "everybody." But often "everybody" means "people like me." When the ride-share service Lyft premiered its new service Lyft Shuttle, which would have replaced individual cars with vans driving on predetermined routes, a Twitter user famously quipped, "That's a bus. You invented a bus." But that's only half the story: Lyft had invented a bus for only people in possession of a smartphone, the savvy to use it, and the credit card to set up the app. You can drop out of college, you can leave your dorm, but the dorm, it seems, will nevertheless haunt your endeavors.

And finally, this elitist anti-elitism has also shaped business practices. In this context, another thinker emerges as central, one who, in fact, is often credited with inspiring Leary's phrase about dropping out. Marshall McLuhan—as unlikely an inspiration as you were going to get—was a literature professor from Toronto who would mix reflections on the *Iliad* with diatribes about the Sunday funnies.

.2.

Content

There's a scene in Woody Allen's *Annie Hall* in which Allen's character and Diane Keaton's character wait in line at a movie theater, while behind them a graying academic type prattles on about Fellini, Bergman, and Marshall McLuhan. Allen's character grows incensed and pleads his case across the fourth wall to the audience. The academic type notices and pushes back: he teaches a class at Columbia and is confident that his insights into McLuhan's work have "a great deal of validity."

Just when you think things can't get any more absurd, Allen pulls from behind a standee the actual Marshall McLuhan, who informs the academic type, "You know nothing of my work." And he adds the supremely mystifying line, "You mean my whole fallacy is wrong."

The scene encapsulates McLuhan's theory rather neatly. McLuhan is famous for the claim that "the medium is the message." What he meant by this is that the way in which radios, TVs, or phones address us is more important than what they say when they do. In this case, Allen is alluding to the fact that film is an interactive medium: we are being addressed not as a remote community, as in a radio broadcast, but instead as direct visual witnesses. Before turning to McLuhan, Allen's character has already made his case, that the guy behind him is a nuisance, across the fourth wall to us filmgoers.

The scene in *Annie Hall* epitomizes how readily available McLuhan's ideas were in the 1960s and '70s. Unless you were an Oscar-winning filmmaker, you couldn't pluck the literal McLuhan out of thin air, of course. But you could certainly invoke his ideas with about as much (apparent) ease. It's safe to say laypeople are less familiar with McLuhan's ideas today than they were then, and it's also safe to say that many who regurgitated his theories, like the gentleman in *Annie Hall*, didn't actually understand them all that well. And given the line the actual McLuhan speaks in the scene, we, the viewers, will likely fear we're misunderstanding him as well.

Did that mean his whole fallacy was wrong? In a way, no, since knowing to invoke McLuhan was perhaps a better proof of his theories than actually understanding those theories. Maybe that is also why Allen left McLuhan's odd line in the final version of the script and the final cut of the film. After all, the point of the scene is that Allen is able to pull the actual McLuhan from behind the standee and have him settle a dispute directly—not what McLuhan actually says, which in no way resolves the dispute. And this was true in the sixties already: invoking McLuhan was a way to show you were switched on, tuned in, vibing, or whatever other media metaphor you want to use to show you've grasped what's happening. You got it, and if you couldn't quite say what *it* was, that mattered less than that you *got* it.

The central way in which the medium can be the message has to do with what it asks us to do, how it asks us to behave toward it. To be addressed as a reader, a listener, an audience member is how human beings are constituted as people in the first place. The medium actively "shapes and controls the scale and form of human association." And in our own age, McLuhan thought, electronic media would eventually create "a small world of tribal drums, total interdependence, and superimposed co-existence." And he didn't seem to dread that idea.

Many other thinkers of the sixties had noticed that TV addressed its audience differently from, say, cinema or the radio. What made McLuhan's theory distinctive was that he didn't bother to ask whether this was a good thing or a bad thing. Media change all the time, and we change with them, and while there is a natural temptation to think that certain forms of media make us *worse* readers, listeners, viewers, the truth is that this kind of value judgment probably makes it hard to really grasp what media are doing. As a literature professor, I interact with a lot of people who try to explain to me why reading on a Kindle, for instance, is intrinsically worse than reading on paper. Maybe that's true, but I've found that this opinion, while widespread, usually depends on (and in turn enables) a pretty distorted caricature of what's involved in reading on an e-reader *or* on paper.

When you read *Understanding Media*, the 1964 book that made McLuhan a household name, it becomes less surprising that people responded to McLuhan in more general rather than specific terms. Because the specifics are strange. McLuhan was a deeply learned man, and he was determined to show it off. That means: lots of allusions, weird digressions, examples that don't seem to illustrate the thing they're supposed to illustrate. To any professor who likes to joke in class, McLuhan's books are painful, not because his jokes are overly recondite, but because they mistake chumminess and condescension for making common cause with their audience. His books careen constantly between things McLuhan was too much of an expert in to pare down and things McLuhan didn't know enough about to understand them himself.

At the same time, McLuhan was a master of the pithy slogan—you may not exactly understand what it means that "man becomes, as it were, the sex organs of the machine world," but you have to admit it's a pretty memorable phrase. He coined terms like "the global village," and "surfing" in the sense that we today "surf" the web—the latter being all the more impressive given that there was no web yet to surf. He himself was surfing on the zeitgeist, which is remarkable: He was trained as a traditional literary critic in the 1930s, and had been teaching at the University of Toronto for two decades by the time he became a star. The books that made him known to non-academic audiences started coming out when McLuhan was already in his fifties. He had, however, been interested for a while in the transition from one media culture to the other—above all, oral culture to literacy, or the advent of print culture. In the sixties he started thinking about his own era along these lines—and about the era that was to come.

We may think that throughout human history, changes are wrought by human beings transforming their world.

But McLuhan proposed that, in fact, history is made by media changing human beings. (For the record, that's what McLuhan means when he says that "man becomes, as it were, the sex organs of the machine world.") Shifts in communication change our way of thinking, our way of relating to one another, our very ways of conceiving of ourselves.

McLuhan is thinking of newly literate Christians poring over the printed Bible in their own language and going to war over what it says. He is thinking of Germans listening to Hitler's voice on the radio. But he's also thinking about the world about to be remade, and about to be made *one world*, by television and electronic media. "Everybody in the world," he proclaimed, in a description that has become only truer every day since, "has to live in the utmost proximity created by our electric involvement in one another's lives." At the same time, McLuhan thought, "electricity does not centralize, but decentralizes." He predicted that unlike newspapers and movies—which draw us into the same streets, theaters, and public squares, where we become a mass and have one unified experience—electronic media would give us similar experiences but by ourselves, or with our own chosen tribe.

McLuhan can feel scarily prescient when you read him in the age of social media bubbles and memes. But when you flip through his writings today, the references feel very of-the-era: Margaret Mead, Carl Jung, Arnold Toynbee. *Understanding Media* is a mid-century modern work. But McLuhan mattered to Silicon Valley not for the way he vibed with Eames chairs and shag carpets but for the way the fifty-something literature professor's Shakespeare-quoting tomes came to resonate with countercultural hipsters half his age. Even by their standards, this adoption was not intuitive. The counterculture's overall image was fairly technophobic, and mass media—especially television—was widely reviled as a tool of conformity and stultification. Nevertheless, something about McLuhan's thought and style caught on. He'd always been a wild and eclectic thinker, his books more collections of essays and thoughts than traditional monographs. So there was a formal fit. But the hippies, or certain hippies, also simply liked what he seemed to be saying.

As Fred Turner has pointed out, *Understanding Media* was a great resource for those members of the counterculture who didn't distrust technology so much as the institutions and state actors that wielded technology. McLuhan preached that media were all-pervasive, inescapable, but increasingly decentralized in a "global village." Media's downstream effects were, in the long run, almost impossible for governments to control. This, as far as the counterculture was concerned, was excellent news. As for the warning that media would eventually transform human consciousness and our very sense of ourselves, well, to sixties rebels this didn't sound like much of a warning. After all, they already wanted to transform consciousness and our sense of self, and they increasingly experienced the failures of mid-century liberalism as a sign that trying to transform consciousness just through content was doomed to fail. Use newspapers to give people good information, and they still won't act on it. But change the tech and you might just change society.

Like many of the invisible prophets of Silicon Valley, McLuhan became important for the tech industry because he allowed his readers to discover a secret structure underneath everyday reality. And because he made it possible to divide the world into those who could discern what was really going on and those who were unable to. The cryptic, at times confusing argument—the phrases that are perhaps more elegant than intelligible—turned out to be a strength rather than a weakness. McLuhan's thoughts suggested that the vast majority of people looked at media, and indeed the world, in a deeply deluded way. Read *Understanding Media* and you'll be privy to an arcane, elite knowledge.

So what exactly is so esoteric about McLuhan's media theory? McLuhan regarded those analysts who focused their attention on the "content" of books or TV shows as dupes: what the medium appeared to say was "like the juicy piece of meat carried by the burglar to distract the watchdog of the mind." The real object of study was the medium itself. But as a result of this—in its way, deeply necessary—adjustment to the way we understand media, a strange new hierarchy snuck into tech discourse. It is impressive how free of value judgment McLuhan's description of media was. It is odd how moralistic the tone in which he framed the shift away from the content was. The medium is for those who get it. The content is for idiots, naïfs, sheep.

McLuhan, for instance, lampoons as "somnambulism" the commonsense assumption that technology "as such" is neither good nor bad, but that it becomes good or bad only in the manner of its use. And he presciently pokes fun at people who say that they personally "pay no attention to ads." Some of this may have been a professor of literature trying hard to unlearn ingrained habits typical of his profession. Some of this may have been a desire to shock. But whatever the reason, content for McLuhan simply wasn't a coequal part of what media were doing. It was a nullity, a distraction.

It's likely that this de-emphasis on content set the tone for the tech industry going forward. The idea that content is in a strange way secondary, even though the platforms Silicon Valley keeps inventing depend on it, is deeply ingrained. And the terms of this value judgment strikingly resemble how McLuhan frames the problem. To *create* content is to be distracted. To *create* the "platform" is to focus on the true structure of reality. Shaping media is better than shaping the content of such media. It is the person who makes the "platform" who becomes a billionaire. The person who provides the content—be it reviews on Yelp, self-published books on Amazon, your own car and waking hours through Uber—is a rube distracted by a glittering but pointless object.

※

McLuhan's culture-defining celebration of media came after decades during which his work was marked by a thoroughgoing pessimism. McLuhan's early work was profoundly weary of modern life, and repulsed by mass media. But when he reinvented himself as a prophet of new media, McLuhan did not abandon his prior pessimistic inclinations: he had been right about postwar culture being mired in a terrible malaise, but now, thanks to new media, culture would finally leave this malaise behind. In this belief, he became useful to Silicon Valley. When his classic works of the sixties address the advent of new media, they sound apocalyptic and excited in equal measure. And why not? He continued to hate the homogeneity peddled by Madison Avenue, comic strips, and Hollywood movies, but he was now hopeful that eventually the changing media landscape would destroy all of that: modernity was terrible, but the new tribal world that would come after was going to be much better.

This way of thinking made McLuhan appealing to the counterculture. But it also ensured that he remained simpatico for the tech industry even as it increasingly left its countercultural origins behind. After all, tech too has a strange optimistic pessimism. Sure, when tech companies make their big announcements, they are all starry-eyed about the future. But when you get right down to it, the industry doesn't have a very high opinion of how things are going. Like the producers of infomercials, tech companies are really good at seeing problems everywhere. The old way of doing X is beset by a host of problems, and product Y can finally solve them all. Where conservative nostalgists discount the present in favor of a radically different past, the tech industry finds the present lacking when compared to the incredible, candy-colored future that is right around the corner. The trick is pure McLuhan.

The more the tech industry sought to take on established, institutional knowledge, the more McLuhan provided its captains with a sense of why establishment forces were debased and not worth saving. McLuhan furnished them with a narrative of historical inevitability, a technological determinism that they could now call on to negate the consequences of their inventions—if it was fated to happen anyway, is it really their fault? Whether it comes to setting down in writing what had previously been passed down orally from generation to generation, or disseminating print to reach, create, and sustain large audiences, there is a sense that once the genie has left the bottle, there's little point to wishing it would go back in.

While when it comes to media such inevitable progress may be plausible and even appealing, a disturbing number of McLuhan's examples are about changes in the business cycle: one group or another being put out of work by technological change. McLuhan seems entirely unconcerned with them—and, to be fair, why should he be? He is a media theorist, not an economist. But it's hard not to get the sense that McLuhan's welcoming attitude toward the apocalyptic changes wrought by media transformation set the tone for the nonchalance with which today's tech companies destroy livelihoods and entire professions in the name of innovation. For us modern readers, the idea that oral culture or manuscript illumination might have deserved to go the way of the dodo seems self-evident. The problem with many of McLuhan's examples is that they transfer that self-evidence onto industries and activities where what counts as progress and superannuation, what counts as necessary advancement and what as a cynical cash grab, is a lot less clear. The very smoothness of the narrative, in other words, becomes a problem.

In the tech industry, this has led to a callousness regarding the communities technology conjures into existence. This isn't to say that it's surprising that a business

would discard its user base if it was no longer profitable—
but it is remarkable how inessential the things happening
on platforms seem to be to the platforms themselves, in
the eyes of both the people working in the upper eche-
lons of these companies and the media covering them.
This is how Tumblr can decide it's getting out of the smut
business, even though it seems to have mostly been about
smut. It probably won't hurt the company's bottom line,
but it does hurt the people who made Tumblr what it was:
the photographers, painters, slash-fic writers, porn cartoonists, and sex workers who had used the platform to
connect safely with an audience. The platform's disregard
for its own content hurts these creators twice: While Tumblr still functioned as their haven, they didn't make nearly
as much money on their creations as the people who created the site that hosted them did. And when it became
politically difficult for Tumblr to remain their haven, they
simply became an afterthought, losing their livelihood and
sometimes even their work itself.

Cartoonists, sex workers, mommy bloggers, book reviewers: there's a pretty clear gender dimension to this divi-
sion of labor. The programmers at Yelp are predominantly
men. Its reviewers are mostly female—and, at least in the
initial years of the company, this was even more true as you
got to the most active "elite" reviewers. Early rewards for
elite reviewers—spa dates and skin care events—suggest
that the company was aware of this and counted on it.
Men build the structures; women fill them. Without users
providing the content, a review portal like Yelp would be
deeply pointless. Nevertheless, the users aren't compensated, or are compensated only with stickers and perks:

their labor is "gamified"; they earn special status or are sent book galleys. The problem isn't that the act of providing content is ignored or uncompensated but rather that it isn't recognized as labor. It is praised as essential, applauded as a form of civic engagement. Remunerated it is not.

The company, the tech, the brand, is about the platform. The content is incidental—in spite of the fact that few people come to a platform for anything but the content. This attitude is reflected in the largely quixotic attempts by users of online platforms to position themselves as employees: In *Tasini et al. v. AOL, Inc. et al.*, a blogger using the now-defunct blog platform of *The Huffington Post* sued for back pay. In a 2013 class action suit brought before the Central District Court of California (*Panzer v. Yelp*), a number of Yelp Elite Squad reviewers charged that they were employees rather than customers. All these claims were eventually dismissed, amid much jeering from the tech press, which called them "frivolous" and "laughable."

From a legal standpoint, these verdicts weren't exactly surprising. But the Stanford researcher Annika Butler-Wall has analyzed the language in which the discourse around these cases was couched and found that articles about the cases actually speak volumes about what counts as "real" labor in tech. Because, sure, these people clearly were not employees in the traditional sense—but the coverage of these lawsuits went further, actually suggesting that what they did wasn't really work, which is another, far more troubling proposition. And deciding what is and isn't work has a long and ignominious history in the United States.

No writer who has ever been encouraged to write for free to "gain exposure" would fail to recognize that this language is on the same spectrum. And no one who has thought about the kinds of labor that habitually go unpaid in our society—affective labor, service, and care work, above all—would fail to recognize that Yelp and AOL are working pretty hard to push what their writers do into that corner. Who knows what gentle disposition moves these good-natured souls to write, what whimsy makes them review restaurants for free? It's not their job; it's a hobby, something to occupy their time. They are "passionate," "supportive" volunteers who want to help other people. These excuses are scripts, in other words, developed around domestic, especially female, labor. To explain why being a mom isn't "real" work. To explain why women aren't worth hiring, or promoting, or paying, or paying as much. Yelp reviewers (again, largely women) usually review service providers (a female-dominated sector of the economy) for a user base that is likely half female—but the people making money on all of it are men.

There are economic reasons behind the fact that very few sites out there pay for content, of course. When you're pitching your startup to a venture capital fund as the next "unicorn," it's better to have a small group of smart programmers you have to compensate than to have a million toiling minions who each might get, or even just plausibly ask for, a piece of the pie. But it isn't just about the vagaries of funding rounds. Silicon Valley seems to genuinely believe in the primacy of the platform. The user has a role to play, but the role is about choosing which platform to be seduced by.

But even if you are lucky enough to receive a paycheck from a tech company, platform fixation affects whether you count as a "tech worker." People in the San Francisco

Bay Area like to yell about all the wealthy Facebook and Google employees who drive up rents and the price of toast. But Facebook and Google employ thousands of cafeteria staff, support staff, security, administrative assistants, and, in the case of Facebook, even parking valets. They employ contingent workers, contractors, and so-called "green-badges" (the color scheme varies from company to company)—people who work at the company and on the product but who are in subtle ways shut out from many of the perks that regularly badged employees enjoy.

Complaints about tech ignore the vast majority of people who make their livelihood, however mediately, from tech. Why? Because these people are not involved with the platform. Because they do not set the parameters by which other people create, share, or market themselves. This is not actually common sense: when people describe the size of the car industry, or of a bank, they include the people who serve the food at the company that makes the rubber for the insulation of the Chevy Tahoe. Being a "tech worker" is somehow more exclusive. Because the platform, and work on it, is more central, more real, than customer relations, or content moderation, or just keeping employees happy.

Toward the end of 2018, a new billboard appeared along Interstate 80 in downtown San Francisco. Put up by a company called Snowflake (according to its Twitter bio, the company offers "a data warehouse built for the cloud"; I have no idea what that means and no intention of finding

out), it exhorted you to be the "boss" of 2019. The tagline?
GRAB 2019 BY THE DATA. The reference seemed clear: Donald Trump's infamous "Grab 'em by the pussy" remark in
the *Access Hollywood* tape. People online debated whether
this trivialized sexual assault, but the bigger Freudian slip
committed by the billboard's ham-fisted joke went largely
unremarked-upon: the strange and pernicious equations
on which a joke like this is built. There is the idea that
running a company resembles being a sexual predator. But
there is also the idea that data—resistant, squirrelly, but
ultimately compliant—is a feminine resource to be seized,
to be made to yield by a masculine force.

To grab data, to dispose of it, to make oneself its
"boss"—the constant onslaught of highly publicized
data breaches may well be a downstream effect of this
kind of thinking. There isn't very much of a care ethic
when it comes to our data on the internet or in the cloud.
Companies accumulate data and then withdraw from it,
acting as though they have no responsibility for it—until
the moment an evil hacker threatens said data. Which
sounds, in other words, not too different from the heavily
gendered imagery relied on by Snowflake. There is no
sense of stewardship or responsibility for the data that
you have "grabbed," and the platform stays at a cool remove from the creaturely things that folks get up to when
they go online and, wittingly or unwittingly, generate
data.

At the same time, withdrawing from content limits your
responsibility. Both legally and morally, content is risky;
the platform is not. The tech industry famously has very
limited legal exposure when it comes to what they put

online—pardon, for what they let others put online. Section 230 of the 1996 Communications Decency Act stipulates that "no provider or user of an interactive computer service shall be treated as the publisher or speaker of any information provided by another information content provider." Another way to put this: a platform is different from a publisher. The latter is editorially responsible for its content; the former is responsible to a much lesser degree.

WordPress is not liable for your blog in the way *The Washington Post* is for your ill-advised editorial. Standing at an Olympian remove from the content, platforms get to claim a neutrality they possess legally but not in actual practice: go on YouTube in private mode and see what the algorithm recommends for you—white supremacist videos, flat-earth conspiracy videos, wild rants about global warming being a hoax. Yet YouTube has convinced not just legislators and lawyers but even its own users that it somehow has less to do with its videos than traditional media companies have to do with their content.

And so, in a strange way, Silicon Valley seems to have learned exactly the lesson it wanted to learn from McLuhan. McLuhan opens *Understanding Media* by saying that the medium is also *socially* the message, meaning that media remake the way groups and classes of people interact, and thus bear enormous responsibility for our discourse, our politics, our commonweal. On the one hand, Silicon Valley has internalized this idea: the means by which information is conveyed does more to our sense of self, to our very personhood, than the information itself. But on the other, the Valley has closed itself to the awesome responsibility that McLuhan imputes to media. In 2019,

Jack Dorsey, the CEO of Twitter, explained in an interview with *Rolling Stone* that the true reason his platform was crawling with Nazi trolls was that users—his customers—were derelict in their duties. "They see things," he complained, "but it's easier to tweet 'get rid of the Nazis' than to report it."

Twitter was happy to take responsibility for Tahrir Square, it seems, but Nazis are someone else's problem. The promotional materials the companies put out claim revolutionary potential for their platforms, but in the end, the tech giants are always happy to get out of jail free by pointing out that they are not responsible for the content on those platforms. There is a tendency in Silicon Valley to want to be revolutionary without, you know, revolutionizing anything.

.3.

Genius

The philosophy of Ayn Rand has long been in league with a certain kind of adolescence. Not adolescence as such, mind you. But an affinity between opinionated youth and Rand's ideas has been something of a constant throughout the nearly eighty years Rand has spent in the American consciousness. All the way back in 1962, Robert L. White, an English professor from Kentucky, called her "a hipster on the right." Even though her acolytes looked nothing like long-haired campus rebels, observers felt that the two rebellions had something in common. And today, many of my more philosophically inquisitive students will cop to having sustained a brief infatuation with Rand in their middle teens. Conversely, many of those who never outgrow her have an immature, autodidactic energy as adults.

Some of this has to do with the philosophy itself. Rand's objectivism proceeds from the premise of an "enlightened self-interest"—even egoism—that is deeply suspicious of any outside influence, whether such influence takes the form of the power or the judgment of other people. The heroes of her novels are young people coming up against traditional structures, which they feel have outlived their usefulness; her villains frequently embody that tradition and have the kind of authority that comes mostly just from age and experience. Her novels are hostile to nuance: characters, institutions, actions fall on one side or the other of a pretty bluntly drawn divide—on the one hand there are creators, on the other there are parasites. It's a factor of the rhetorical magic of her books that readers are not only always on the side of the creators—they are by some kind of participatory reading automatically *part* of the creators.

It is a common suggestion that Rand's novels are perhaps better treatises than works of literature; that the plots are pretty threadbare attempts to maneuver Rand's mouthpieces into position to hold forth, for page upon page, about the virtues of selfishness. This view can obscure the fact that these books can really function only as novels. They aren't manifestos that loosely wear the costume of a baggy novel; they are manifestos that cannot work unless they wear that costume. A vaguely novelistic understanding of the world is central to her philosophy. Rand thinks through storytelling, and she has woven herself into the way Silicon Valley tells stories about itself.

Rand presents a world in which self-reliance is easy and pure. And her work depends on an understanding of self-reliance that doesn't really stand up to scrutiny once you've had to, you know, actually self-rely. She is an absolutist about things that are clearly socially conditioned, which can give her world a kind of taxidermic feel. She celebrates capitalist enterprise while ignoring the communal and moral frameworks that it presupposes in order to function. Her fiction is almost entirely about the world of adult workplaces—architecture firms, boardrooms—but it seems to have a purely aesthetic view of what work is all about. There are many moments in *Atlas Shrugged* (1957) and *The Fountainhead* (1943) in which the fun house version of capitalist society presented in these books comes into gorgeous, bizarre focus. Consider the moment when the all-powerful architecture critic (yes, you read that right) Ellsworth Toohey, who is a Marxist and also in league with monopoly capitalists and also beloved by the populace, schemes to take over Gail Wynand's newspaper, the *Banner,* on the strength of (and I'm not making this up) his writing a column in it. The right pieces are there, but they hang together in baffling ways—like an economic system dreamed up by Borges.

It's not shocking that Rand's writing would appeal to people whose work is imposed by parents, who fancy themselves individualists but aren't allowed to drive themselves to school yet. But the fact that Ayn Rand's philosophy resonates with adolescents in important ways should not hide the fact that this alliance is forged by a savvy bit of marketing. Young people are drawn to Ayn Rand because Ayn Rand is marketed to young people. Since the 1980s, the Ayn Rand Institute in Irvine, California, has run the Ayn Rand essay contests for high school students—more recent versions have included options for college students as well. If you had the right high school teacher, you've encountered the contests: answer a question about one of Rand's books in six hundred to sixteen hundred words and you could win $25,000 (if you place first in the *Atlas Shrugged* category; strangely enough, *Anthem* nets you only $2,000). Interestingly, techies are not well represented among the winners. Perhaps tech has graduated from Ayn

Rand the same way it graduates from the university—you grab a few ideas and you're on your way.

Like many of the philosophies considered in this book, Rand's feel very specific to a certain time and place but have been preserved in some pockets of American society. Unlike the ideas of McLuhan, the information theorist Claude Shannon, or the economist Joseph Schumpeter, however, people still very much remember where these ideas come from. In fact, until the Republican Party abandoned Randianism for white nationalism in 2016, Rand's ideas had arguably had a better run in the twenty-first century than in the twentieth. At the same time, it's worth remembering where they first emerged from.

Rand arrived in the United States in the mid-1920s, having finished her studies in the Soviet Union, and ended up in Hollywood, where she worked different jobs around the studios and began writing screenplays. From the first, then, her conservatism was that of an outsider and that of an artist. Rand's profound suspicion of what Howard Roark in *The Fountainhead* would call "second-handers"—people who get ahead on the strength of ideas and privileges given to them by others—reflected both her jealousy vis-à-vis a perceived establishment and the fact that this jealousy was not so much about material goods as aesthetic matters—taste, prestige, recognition. Rand's first novel, never published during her lifetime, is about an actress. Her first published books, *We the Living* (1936) and *Anthem* (1938), took up the topic of totalitarianism. Neither was a major success.

Books like *Anthem* became legion in the 1940s and '50s. Books that rebelled against the conformism of middle-class, mid-century America, that echoed the anticommunism of those years, and that combined these two in the intuition that conformism was somehow in league with FDR's New Deal. But compared to books like Ray Bradbury's *Fahren-heit 451* (1953) and Robert Heinlein's *The Moon Is a Harsh Mistress* (1966), Rand's anarchism is downbeat. After all, to her, totalitarianism was not theoretical in the least; it had displaced her family and almost prematurely cut short her education. Equality 7-2521, the narrator of *Anthem*, ends his reflections wondering

> how it was possible, in those graceless years of transition, long ago, that men did not see whither they were going, and went on, in blindness and cowardice, to their fate. I wonder, for it is hard for me to conceive how men who knew the word "I" could give it up and not know what they lost.

Rand fused the fear of collectivism with a kind of lost-cause conservatism that was generally popular during the "wilderness years," the time between 1932 and 1968 in which conservatives found themselves generally out of step with the American mainstream. Conservatism during those years consisted, as the critic Lionel Trilling wrote in 1950, less of ideas than of "irritable mental gestures which seek to resemble ideas." Such gestures of retreat, melancholia, isolation, and a serious persecution complex are all over Rand's fiction and public persona. Gestures of revulsion and disgust, gestures that combine schoolyard taunts and a pretty thin skin.

⠐⠔

Silicon Valley's youth obsession has allowed Rand's ideas to thrive in an environment that would on first glance seem politically inimical. Whenever Rand rears her head in Silicon Valley, it's not so much in the form of an idea but in the "irritable mental gestures" seeking to resemble ideas that Trilling wrote about. And it is in unexpected places. Certainly, there are dyed-in-the-wool objectivists in the tech industry. There's Peter Thiel, who seems to have grown up on a mix of *Atlas Shrugged* and *The Silmarillion*; there's Sam Altman of Y Combinator fame; there's Travis Kalanick, whose Twitter avatar used to be the cover of *The Fountainhead*. There's Steve Jobs, who was inspired by Rand in his youth, according to his Apple cofounder, Steve Wozniak. But far more frequently, Rand's ideas have started wearing the native garb of Northern California. They come with the crunchy flavor of the counterculture; they talk about team-building and making the world a better place.

The problem-solving acumen of Elon Musk, for instance, speaks to the billionaire's sense of responsibility toward others and his planet. But it is always also animated by a kind of impatience with governments, with experts, with any large collective group having an accumulated sense of how best to do certain things. Rather than let cave divers strategize, based on past experience, how to rescue some kids from a cave in Thailand, Musk will come up with a robot that'll do them one better, and he'll do it all by himself. Musk, in other words, pulled off the seemingly impossible trick of giving compassion a Randian hue.

Ever wonder what philosophy animates popular Pixar

films like *The Incredibles*, *Ratatouille*, and *Wall-E*? Think of young Dash Parr (the Incredibles' son) being told that "everyone is special" and harrumphing that that's "another way of saying no one is." About the idea that it is the business of special people to be special, and of their lessers to get out of their way. *The Incredibles* is kind of admirable for the bluntness with which it advocates that inequality is natural, or deserved, and should be affirmed. Pixar films, especially the ones directed by Brad Bird, frequently mimic Rand's tendency to have her villains pander down to the masses and up to the financial, academic, and taste-making elite at once.

But that message gets mixed with other trace elements characteristic of the hippiefied version of Rand you see in the colorful office parks along U.S. 101. In *Ratatouille* it's the enduring myth of self-realization. *Ratatouille* is about a rat who wants to be a chef, and who is in fact a natural talent. But he's also, you know, a rat—his entire clan of rats like to stuff themselves with garbage, and he's up against a snobby gatekeeper critic named Anton Ego. The film's ethos is encapsulated by the famed chef Auguste Gusteau claiming "anyone can cook"; and the main character, Remy, spends the entire film proving himself Gusteau's worthy, if unlikely, successor. But the film is deceptive, for *Ratatouille* proves Gusteau's words only by tweaking them. In reality, the film is saying that if you're a super-special rat with God-given talent, you ought to be treated like the genius you are, no matter who you are. In the end, Ego probably summarizes the film's central premise better: "Not everyone can become a great artist. But a great artist can come from anywhere."

Again and again, Pixar indulges the tropes of flip-flop-wearing Northern California but ends up with something that sounds a lot like Ayn Rand. For a big-budget Disney production, *Wall-E* gets pretty brutal in its takedown of consumer capitalism. Thanks to the efforts of a giant corporation, Buy n Large, humanity has been reduced to large indolent blobs, driving around in jazzy chairs in a Carnival Cruise–style spaceship, waited on by subservient robots. But you get the sense that the film doesn't direct its anger toward the big, bad corporation behind it all—instead, it spends most of its time lampooning the consumers who allowed themselves to be brainwashed by it. The cultural critic and blogger Mark Fisher has called this the film's "gestural anti-capitalism," and it is characteristic of Silicon Valley Randians: they are disgusted not so much by the manipulators as by the manipulated. This is how tech entrepreneurs like Peter Thiel manage to be both vocal opponents of elites and hugely elitist: if you're dumb enough to buy what I'm selling, he seems to think, you really shouldn't be voting.

Even when Silicon Valley went all in on Bernie Sanders's presidential campaign in 2016, a lot of the techies seemed to profoundly misunderstand the senator from Vermont. You'd talk to self-declared Bernie Bros (a label that Sanders's core supporters tended to be leery of applying to themselves) at tech parties and they'd talk about how Sanders would shake up the establishment and make it easier to innovate. And you'd have to wonder what the hell they were hearing when they were listening to the man who never made any bones about his frosty relationship to American capitalism. Sure, Sanders was looking to disrupt government—but in the direction of more government, something that at least some of his fans in Redwood City, Palo Alto, and Mountain View seemed to miss.

Unlike the strange alliance objectivist thinking forged with young people who look and behave like old people, these hippie admixtures are not strategic. They have to do with how Ayn Rand arrived in Silicon Valley, namely via the sixties counterculture. While Rand had nothing but disdain for the young radicals of the counterculture ("savages" seems to have been her favorite put-down for them), some parts of the counterculture embraced Rand's books. This is probably because they encountered Rand as a novelist. Rand the political thinker was either largely unavailable or largely uninteresting to them. When the generation that coined the slogan "Trust no one over thirty" read *Atlas Shrugged*, the objectivist writer Jeff Riggenbach points out, "they found nothing in it to dissuade them from this prejudice."

The communication scholar Jonathan Taplin has suggested that tech started out as a project of sweet countercultural hippies, only to later be hijacked by a "libertarian counterinsurgency." The counterculture as we like to remember it (and as its contemporaries perhaps liked to imagine it) was certainly opposed to a me-first faith in markets and corporations. But the counterculture also always had its other side. In *The Conquest of Cool* (1997), the journalist Thomas Frank has outlined the many ways in which we go wrong when we assume that the counterculture had a period of authenticity and was subsequently co-opted by the suits, the culture industry, and corporate America. In truth, much of the counterculture was dependent on big business. Sure, it could warn against people who bowed and prayed to the neon god they made, but it did so on an LP released by Columbia Records and later in a film that cost Embassy Pictures the equivalent of twenty million present-day dollars.

A lot of the counterculture also led to the formation of big business. Especially in California, distrust of the government and disgust with COINTELPRO and the war in Vietnam frequently translated into a conviction that perhaps business was the more natural, spontaneous form of human self-organization, and was actually less prone to abuse and tyranny than government. And while the hippies fully understood they couldn't run the government in faraway Washington, the world of business seemed more decentralized and more porous. The signifiers of the counterculture, and often its protagonists themselves, took over entire industries, generating massive profits in the process.

And a lot of communes either functioned as, or transitioned into, highly profitable businesses. Stewart Brand's *Whole Earth Catalog*, a quirky countercultural compendium marketing DIY solutions, which Steve Jobs once credited as a forerunner to Google, was modeled on the L.L.Bean catalog. The vision was self-renewal and self-reliance through the magic of the right tool. Doesn't all of this sound fairly simpatico with what Rand was selling? So, however much Rand hated the counterculture, Riggenbach is probably right that at least certain parts of it were anything but allergic to her ideas. This was particularly true when Rand's novels treated capitalist enterprise as a form of free self-expression.

The Fountainhead, for instance, is at its heart an artist

novel, even though the artistry in question expresses itself in cranes, concrete mixers, and steel girders. The artists in it paint on a canvas normally reserved for large corporations, and they seem to do so without the distortion a collective enterprise like a corporation usually introduces. Conversely, the wealthy industrialists portrayed in the novel are treated like either failed, frustrated, or fulfilled artists of commerce.

There's Guy Francon, whose business ventures follow the whims of society and who projects no values of his own. There's Hopton Stoddard, who is beset by guilt over his own success, which the villainous Toohey exploits to talk him into various contributions to charitable causes. Similarly, the publisher Gail Wynand is a typical Randian nihilist—he makes money even with things he knows to be trash, and completely comes apart when he realizes that he could have made his fortune following his own instincts rather than those of the masses. In other words, these businesses do not function in the way businesses tend to function in the real world—they exist as aesthetic creations and as methods of self-realization. In Rand, corporations are self-portraiture.

There are few novels that weave as effortlessly between the founding and failure of architectural companies and interpersonal melodrama as *The Fountainhead*, and indeed the book seems at times incapable of distinguishing one from the other. There are few novels with this many devious building commissions and Machiavellian architectural critics. Buildings are built and torn down with such swiftness that it's easy to get the sense that architecture is a kind of bizarre stand-in for far less communal

efforts. But the novel acknowledges as much in its climac-
tic confrontation between the brilliant individualist Roark
and the talentless follower Peter Keating: Keating comes to
Roark with a commission he cannot himself make good
on, and Roark agrees to design the building using his
frequently attested-to brilliance and let Keating take the
credit. But, he demands, Keating must build the building
exactly as Roark designs it.

In other words, there is a weird (and acknowledged)
tendency here to treat an effort like architecture, which by
definition requires a group and—dare I say it—collectives,
as though it were the art that an individual makes in the
solitude of a studio or a favorite writing nook. This is what
historians of ideas call a "genius aesthetic": it describes
our tendency to think that the meaning of a work of art
comes out of the specific mind of its creator, not out of
the preexisting rules that creator worked within nor the
broader spirit of the society and time. When you're talking
about a novel, that makes a certain amount of sense. But
Rand extended this sense of individual brilliance to some
of humanity's most communal undertakings. Have you
ever looked at a rail line and thought, I wonder what the
one genius who decided to build a bridge over this valley was thinking? Rand has. And notice that, thanks to
Elon Musk, we actually finally do have a billionaire whose
weird tunnel-boring projects are basically a form of performance art—a pure emanation of individual genius, and
sort of useless to anyone else.

As the political scientist Corey Robin points out, Rand
grew up wanting to write screenplays and honed her craft

as a writer in Hollywood. The film industry is one of those rare examples where legions of anonymous writers, set designers, sound mixers, and technicians, many of them well organized in unions, create an aesthetic object, and in the end that object says it's, for example, "a Damien Chazelle film." And while Rand's cyclopean novels seem miles away from the efficient entertainments of the multiplex, their melodramatic turns are clearly inspired by Hollywood: her villains are ravishing mustachio-twirlers; her heroes are resplendent and incorruptible; there's just one nefarious plot after the other, and then a full vindication of the hero.

Rand's heroic individualism has become an inescapable part of how the tech industry presents itself. Through her genius aesthetic, the very *unaesthetic* practice of coding (if you don't believe me, any time a TV show tries to make computer hacking *look* exciting, remind yourself what it would *actually* look like to watch someone do this) could be turned into a manly struggle. Through it, people with the good fortune of having invested in the right idea at the right time, or having been roommates with the right person freshman year, or having had cash to spread around at the right moment, become tech messiahs with followers hanging on to their every word.

Just about anyone actually working in tech will tell you that's a massive distortion of reality. Work in tech is almost always teamwork; it often doesn't look nearly as cool as the things it can make happen; and in the end, if you take away the colorful bikes and the free burritos, it is a job like any other. But the point is that, to both the outside world and their own employees, tech companies clearly want to present it as not just another job. The aestheticization of labor is perhaps the central distinguishing feature of the tech job, and it has turned tech into the leading indicator for what work is like today.

But something similar actually applies to the other end of the tech-employment spectrum. Because while the people writing the code are encouraged to think of themselves not so much as workers but as part of a family, the people being sent to drive for Uber, deliver Amazon products, or pick up food for DoorDash are told they are not employees. The gig economy itself is an aestheticization of labor practices. Sure, what you're doing may look a whole lot like what a pizza delivery guy did twenty years ago, but what you're really doing is (according to ads looking to reel in new DoorDash drivers) being your own boss, exploring new parts of the city, paying for your wedding.

Equality 7-2521, the narrator of *Anthem*, writes reflections in defiance of the conventions of his entirely collectivized society. The entire novel we're reading is an act of heresy, and the heretical thrill we may feel at reading the novel's unpopular warnings is perhaps supposed to be a distant echo of Equality 7-2521's bravery. Toward the end of his narrative, Equality 7-2521 wonders about how the word "I,"

and the concept of the self as something worth asserting and defending, first disappeared from thinking:

> Perhaps, in those days, there were a few among men, a few of clear sight and clean soul, who refused to surrender that word. What agony must have been theirs before that which they saw coming and could not stop! Perhaps they cried out in protest and in warning. But men paid no heed to their warning. And they, these few, fought a hopeless battle, and they perished with their banners smeared by their own blood. And they chose to perish, for they knew.

There is an entire genre of dystopias in which things we take for granted have been banned: feelings, reading, being Dauntless and Erudite at the same time. They can feel a little bit silly, but the trope derives at least part of its effectiveness from the fact that it ennobles some of our most quotidian actions, turning them into grand gestures of rebellion and courage. This is particularly true of books that congratulate you for reading books—which *Anthem* fairly explicitly does. But Rand's novel doesn't stop there: by the time you're done with Equality 7-2521's chronicle, you will be inclined to applaud yourself for not surrendering the word "I," for thinking that people are coming for it, and for refusing to let go of the tenth most frequently used word in the English language. For knowing that those who are coming for it will gore you and smear your banners with your blood.

The (famously grumpy) German cultural critic Theodor W. Adorno wrote in the 1940s that "in many people it is already an impertinence to say 'I.'" Around the same time, Rand's *Anthem* proposed that it was in fact already a revolution to say "I." Both Adorno and Rand were profoundly worried about the rise of totalitarianism in the mid-twentieth century. But where Adorno thought this meant that resisting society's tendency toward conformity and totalization was an extremely hard thing to do, Rand implicitly lowered the bar for what counts as resistance.

Rand's kind of resistance doesn't require you to change the way you live your life; it doesn't require you to grapple with a completely new picture of the world. It requires you to do what you're already doing, but now with the added halo of the political. Don't like paying your taxes? Well, good news, that's now an ideological stance. Annoyed by bureaucracy and tedious meetings? Well, congrats, because that's philosophy now. This is the genius behind the kvetching about "political correctness," for instance: you get to keep talking the way you've always talked, but instead of having to worry you're being lazy, you get to tell yourself you're actually being courageous.

The genius aesthetic that rules the tech industry relies again and again on this purely gestural kind of courage, on hyping everyday things into grand acts of nonconformism and even resistance. You repeat what people around you are saying anyway and get to call yourself a freethinker. You invest other people's money to make use of other people's labor, and you get to call yourself a risk-taker. You tell your coworkers that they really shouldn't be your coworkers, then you go on Tucker Carlson and talk about

persecution. And with this sort of courage, which consists only of gestures of courage, comes a communication that likewise just goes through the motions. If this
chapter was about what a certain genius aesthetic sees as
courage and independence, then the next will be about
the disappointment that occupies the gap between the aes-
theticized simulacrum and the genuine article.

.4.

Communication

"From family to nation, every human group is a society of island universes," Aldous Huxley wrote in 1954. "We live together, we act on, and react to, one another; but always and in all circumstances we are by ourselves. The martyrs go hand in hand into the arena; they are crucified alone." Huxley strove to overcome this condition, to attain greater empathy, to resonate with others on a more profound level. To know the inner states of others through more than mere inference, through analogy with one's own self. He sought it through Vedanta, through meditation, through LSD, and—as in the episode described below—through mescaline.

In most cases, however, Huxley came away disappointed. When he gulped down a cup of water with 0.4 grams of mescaline, he says in *The Doors of Perception* (1954), "I was convinced in advance that the drug would admit me . . . into the kind of inner world described by Blake," that he would be able to see the world through the eyes of the mystics, of Johann Sebastian Bach. Mescaline, it turned out, was not the way to make that happen. But by a circuitous route, Huxley's vision of a mind-meld accomplished by new technologies and subtended by a rejection of Western understandings of the mind was transmitted to the tech industry.

In 1960, a Stanford graduate named Dick Price attended a Huxley lecture titled "Human Potentialities." In

1962, along with another Stanford graduate, Michael Murphy, and with the support of various Northern California intellectuals, including Frederic Spiegelberg (a scholar of Eastern religions at Stanford), the anthropologist Gregory Bateson, and Fritz Perls (most famous for the idea of Gestalt therapy), Price opened the Esalen Institute in Big Sur, along the California coast. Huxley soon began giving lectures and seminars at Esalen, as did luminaries such as R. Buckminster Fuller, Ken Kesey, Linus Pauling, and Joseph Campbell. Esalen became known as a center for the human potential movement, one of the longest-lasting institutions of New Age spiritualism.

In recent years, Esalen has come under the sway of Silicon Valley—its current CEO came from the Wikimedia Foundation, and the institute offers courses in "Designing the Life We Want" taught by Silicon Valley consultants. But this isn't the first time the meditating hippies of the central coast and the Bay Area techies have met. It's just that for a long time, the influence went primarily the other way. During Esalen's first, most vibrant decade, academics across America were working on ARPANET, the forerunner of the internet. The first message sent via a wide area network, in 1969, went between a lab at the Stanford Research Institute and one at UCLA. As the American historian Peter N. Miller points out, Stanford's d.school, which focuses on product design and has helped define the tech industry's approach to gadgets, user experience, and the creative process, was shaped by people with Esalen connections.

And while meditation and yogic practices were the institute's primary foci, technology was part of the bargain from the start. What else, after all, were 0.4 grams of mescaline dissolved in tap water if not a technology for throwing open the doors of perception? You can get a sense for just how much tech savvy, and how much faith in technology, the human potential movement had, from a story related by the historian (and Esalen board member) Jeffrey Kripal: In 1982, the Russian-American Center (TRAC) at Esalen undertook an experiment in citizen diplomacy. Steve Wozniak, of Apple fame, helped them establish the first satellite communications between the Soviet Union and the United States, allowing citizens, rather than governments, to communicate directly. The first event, Kripal points out, was pretty telling in the way it combined counterculture with then-cutting-edge tech: a set of concerts in a "Satellite Rock-and-Roll Fest."

But if Huxley's stratospheric hopes for his mescaline experience traveled from Esalen and other countercultural institutions to the garages and office parks between Redwood City and Mountain View, Huxley's sense of disappointment traveled along with them. The counterculture furnished techies with a bold intuition of what was possible in communication—and a prefabricated sense of letdown when actual human communication once again fell short of the experiences imagined as you reached for the glass of water with mescaline in it.

And the thing is, we know both of these feelings only too well. On the one hand, there's the incredible sense of potential when we're suddenly connected to a much wider world in ways that even twenty years ago would have seemed hopelessly futuristic. And on the other hand, there's the feeling that we keep messing it up, that maybe our communication media are such spam-filled, dick-pic-laden, Nazi-promoting cesspools because we're somehow doing them wrong. This chapter isn't about the incredible promise of consciousness expansion that our new communication technologies, often quite justifiably, fuel. It is about our disappointment with them and the uses to which that disappointment has been put.

Marshall McLuhan appears to have been critical of what came to be popularized as the Shannon-Weaver model of communication, as well as of Norbert Wiener's cybernetics, because they paid insufficient attention to "how people are changed by the instruments they employ." In a strange way, McLuhan and Claude Shannon predicted the two central features that define our twenty-first-century media landscape. Shannon pointed out that by the management of redundancy, almost any content could be beamed across the planet. And McLuhan sensed that, because people would be producing, receiving, and enjoying that content, they would load up every available channel with redundancy right away. In other words: we *can* communicate better, and therefore we will actually communicate worse.

This isn't exactly a new problem. In his book *Speaking into the Air*, John Durham Peters argues that "communication" has always been a concept that brims with potential, a potential that actual acts of communication nearly always fall short of. There is an almost mystical fantasy of perfect transparency, community, and directness behind this concept that draws on imagery of religious visions and divine inspiration. Though the word is quite old, the concept of communication became compelling to philosophers and theorists only once it was both imperative that messages travel with little distortion and clear that they very rarely did. The concept designates, as Peters puts it, both a bridge and a barrier. Or, put another way, communication was often taken to be solving the problems communication had created in the first place.

This has allied both the problem and the promise of communication with technological progress. The more networked we become, for instance, the more abuse of our systems of communication becomes a dangerous issue. Fake news on social media matters a great deal more than, say, a monk writing a fake chronicle in twelfth-century England, or someone drawing a slanderous cartoon in eighteenth-century France. But the fact that discourse about communication has traditionally pulled from mystical or religious language has allowed the media of the internet age to hide behind a convenient sense of disappointment—a dodge that has shadowed acts of communication since well before Huxley took his first gulp of mescaline. As a result, we aren't able to communicate very well about our systems of communication.

If you require documentation for that claim, simply ask @jack—the Twitter CEO, Jack Dorsey—about banning neo-Nazis from his platform. You'll get back an ever-changing cloud of verbiage, abuzz with ideals and high hopes. He'll elide the fact that in countries where showing certain content would expose Twitter to legal liability, the company is perfectly happy to let those ideals and hopes be damned and get busy censoring. He'll elide the incredibly tricky and deeply political choices his company makes to decide what content to take down. He'll even elide exactly how this is done. At most, you get a sense of profound disappointment: We built you kids this amazing toy, and all you can think to do with it is be Nazis or call each other Nazis. This, as people so often remark on @jack's platform, is why we can't have nice things.

This space of disappointment is one that the right and the left, capitalists and their Marxist critics, largely occupy together, at times quite amicably. The company Palantir Technologies is universally regarded as one of the more dangerous in Silicon Valley when it comes to the possible violation of civil rights and threats to free speech. It creates technologies that aggregate and cross-reference massive data banks and try to predict threats to national security or whether, you know, an individual is an undocumented immigrant. And independent of whether you like the idea of the NSA or the FBI having access to such technologies, other companies have already created tech for far more authoritarian governments.

Two of the founders of Palantir are Peter Thiel and Alex Karp. Karp is a rarity among Silicon Valley CEOs, as he has a Ph.D. in social theory, having studied with Jürgen Habermas. (His dissertation adviser was another Frankfurt professor, Karola Brede, who isn't nearly as well-known and whom Karp usually doesn't mention.) This is often noted as something of a contradiction: Karp likes to invoke Habermas, one of the great theorists of the liberal order and of rights and transparency, yet he now builds technologies widely seen as being deeply dangerous to all of those things. Palantir Technologies, after all, is named after the great seeing stones of Tolkien's *The Lord of the Rings*—like them, its technology is meant to allow the powerful to see what others cannot. That kind of imbalance contradicts the central idea of a public sphere, which, according to Habermas, we are all supposed to enter as equals. And yet, it isn't as though Habermas were altogether bullish on the public sphere. In his great book *The Structural Transformation of the Public Sphere* (1962), he instead traces a gradual decline of the public sphere under pressure from mass media and consumer culture. While Habermas is not a cultural pessimist, he uses a narrative of decline characteristic of cultural pessimism. The public sphere is an ideal, and we've spent the last two hundred years falling increasingly short of it.

Karp's dissertation uses the work of the sociologist Talcott Parsons to analyze what he calls "jargon"—speech that is used more for the feelings it engenders and transports in certain quarters than for its informational content; it's language that, in a sense, makes its home in the space between the promises of the public sphere and its actuality. His example is a speech by the German author Martin Walser complaining about a supposed social compulsion in Germany to constantly refer back to the Holocaust and to Nazi crimes. Karp asserts right off the bat that the compulsion is essentially an imaginary one—but then wants to know *why* Walser imagined it, and why his imagining of it caught on. His answer is a critique of political correctness: while the facts weren't on Walser's side, he was giving expression to the sense that "respect for certain social taboos and the ritualization of cultural messaging [around them] ultimately constitute a disparagement of the call that is within each human being: to judge over right and wrong according to his own conscience."

Karp's dissertation is from 2002. And yet it suggests so much about how Silicon Valley views more recent questions concerning communication and the public sphere. Interestingly enough, Karp never actually makes the critique I just imputed to him: he tiptoes up to the line of claiming for Walser a right to transgress for the sake of transgressing, a right to rebel against strictures of decorum—a sensibility that we would today identify as trolling. And then he moves on to his works cited. Was Walser right? Was his speech an example of the public sphere working as intended, or a sign of social cohesion around public expression beginning to fray? Instead of answering, Karp cuts to the credits. Although Karp wrote the dissertation shortly before he transitioned to Silicon Valley, his dissertation already had one discursive gambit of the tech industry exactly right: a curious refusal of confrontation. Peter Thiel is fond of joking that "competition is for losers," and in the marketplace of ideas, Silicon Valley seems to largely agree with him.

Silicon Valley has a habit of pretending to have a debate when in fact desiring no such thing. One version of this is reflected in the infamous "Google memo" that James Damore uploaded to a Google internal mailing list in July 2017, and which quickly leaked to the media. In the memo, Damore argued against diversity efforts at the company, essentially suggesting that lack of representation at Google, especially of women and people of color, was the result of biological factors rather than discrimination or structural inequality. The memo caused an immediate uproar. Damore was eventually fired, and has since made having been fired his full-time job. Writing in *The New York Times*, the columnist and professional tone policeman David Brooks framed the fracas as one huge disappointment: "What we have is a legitimate tension," he suggested, and lamented that our public discourse lacked the subtlety to reconcile it. Many commentators on the right echoed his hand-wringing about the fact that we "no longer" had the shared framework to debate the vital issues of the day. What they missed (probably often intentionally) was that the Google memo didn't fall victim to the lack of a shared neutral framework but rather exploited the absence of one.

It's worth parsing out the rhetorical gestures in this document—because Damore is good at making it look like he is doing something without actually doing it. And people like Brooks—who isn't the most careful reader on his best of days—were determined to believe the document actually intervened in some debate rather than exploited the fact that there was no other reaction Damore's intervention could have elicited. According to the memo, titled "Google's Ideological Echo Chamber," Damore wants to advance the health of the company and, indeed, society. In a handy chart, Damore juxtaposes progressive and conservative personality types, which he extends to societies and companies. "A company too far to the right may be slow to react, overly hierarchical, and untrusting of others."

Damore is very careful to hedge: after dividing people, societies, and companies along these axes, he allows that "neither side is 100% correct and both viewpoints are necessary for a functioning society or, in this case, company." So is the "ideological echo chamber" mentioned in the memo's title a problem because it hampers the company from functioning properly? (Google is currently valued at around \$730 billion; one wonders what it would be worth if functioning properly.) Or because it would finally make more pragmatic a company that's famous for dreaming up things people couldn't have conceived of even a decade prior? Or because it is unfair to treat more pragmatically minded people differently, just because a company is idealistic?

Every one of these readings is possible, and none of them make any sense. Damore can't say whether he's making a normative or pragmatic argument, whether he is making one that concerns society in general or the company he works at in particular. He can't say whether he's standing up for the company as a whole or for individual people working there. He can't say how conservative business practices are supposed to be analogous to conservative personality structures. But perhaps more important than the fact that he can't is the fact that he badly wants to.

In general, the memo seems intent on having the meanings of words carry over from use to use in ways that are almost impossible. It charts a juxtaposition such as "Change is good (unstable)" versus "Change is dangerous (stable)," and then plugs anything and everything into that matrix. Is a person who thinks that it's good to shake up a teachers' union really a "progressive"? Isn't a person who wants his employer to get rid of all contraceptive coverage being idealistic rather than pragmatic? The point here isn't that Damore's chart makes little sense. It's that any sense it does make is made only when words are forced to retain their uses and definitions well beyond the limits of what everyday experience teaches us can be expected.

So whatever we want to say about the Google memo, we can say that David Brooks had it wrong. It's not that poor James Damore made an honest overture to the closed-minded (but "unstable") libs and they turned on him. It's that he sent a message meant to be misunderstood. To engage with it at all is to get tripped up in its terminology, to chafe against assumptions it has to make but won't acknowledge. The real point of the message is the inevitable next step, where the writer claims that his text—which, recall, is pretty much impossible to make sense of on its own terms—was unfortunately and woefully misunderstood. The memo exists to allow David Brooks to be sad about it. Damore's missive is not a communication that's sent out into the world by someone hoping to be understood by an audience. It is a communication sent out by someone in order to be disappointed, an offering to be refused.

But here's the thing: James Damore is fairly typical in his occupying and weaponizing that space of preordained, deliberately engineered disappointment. We have all been there. We all send this missive, we all know the joy of being disappointed, at least some of the time. It's the feeling of having tried to communicate honestly but the other side is just too darn ideological to genuinely engage. I don't mean to suggest that this feeling is never correct or appropriate—rather that we over-rely on it and are falsely deferential to it, even when it isn't correct or appropriate. After all, some version of this feeling is inherent in all trolling: I tried to engage with this question in good faith, and my opponents decided to be uncivil.

Or think of the species known as the "reply-guy"— someone who replies to a tweet or a Facebook post that seemed to require no reply, and who then invariably expresses disappointment when the original poster tells him so. The original poster shares an experience, and the reply-guy tries to suggest that the original poster might not actually have experienced what he or she experienced. Maybe the racism you encountered wasn't really racism? Maybe you need a dude in your mentions to explain your own terms to you? Maybe bringing this back to all lives mattering would help the discussion?

One thing that both troll and reply-guy cannot usually explain is what result their intervention was supposedly intended to elicit. They know only that the actual result of their intervention is deeply disappointing to them and flies in the face of the good faith effort they made in responding to the original post. The Google memo is caught in this same ambiguity: How did Damore think Google should respond to his memo? What was the reception he was hoping for, in comparison with which its actual reception was so brutally disappointing? These are questions that really should be part of any communication one initiates. But it is noticeable that when one renders absolute the value of communication as such, particular questions like these can become obscured.

The problem is not that promises of communication are overly idealistic. It's that the thinking about communication gets to hide behind its own idealism—gets to hide how we make meaning and what we communicate when we do communicate. As Peters points out, this stance is easy to confuse with modes of interrogation that have come to define what Europeans and Americans have traditionally thought of as solid argumentation: parrhesia, speaking truth to power, the Socratic method, the test by ridicule.

But trolling abandons both the shared purpose of a communication (to convince one another, to engage in dialogue) and the shared audience to which both you and the person challenging you want to appeal. What remains is the cynical subject, as Peters describes it: "cool, aloof, and self-contained." The troll is in control of when you lose control.

The philosopher Peter Sloterdijk once described modern cynicism as enlightened false consciousness: we are able to get by acting as though we believe in things we don't. Painting the troll as the ultimate cynic, as Peters does, or as heir to a long line of heretics, as the journalist Angela Nagle does in her book *Kill All Normies* (2017), is both accurate and perhaps a bit too generous. Peters and Nagle certainly capture one aspect of what trolling is, but in central respects the troll is a cynic who represses the fact that he is a cynic. The cynics of antiquity were the natural foes of the authority of tradition. The supposed traditions their postmodern heirs delight in attacking are women writing in traditionally masculine domains, political correctness, trans people being treated as people. The somewhat older traditions of white supremacy, androcentrism, and eurocentrism they are content to leave standing. And the supposed traditions and orthodoxies they like to pick on do not enjoy broad legitimacy across the West, let alone the world. One could be forgiven, in other words, for suspecting the trolls of 4chan and Reddit of making a fairly clear argument. Our ironists, it turns out, are faithful people.

Nagle's *Kill All Normies* expresses profound bafflement as to how "the culture of 4chan, Anonymous etc., in the pre-gamergate days" eventually came to be characterized "by a particularly dark preoccupation with thwarted or failed white Western masculinity." Nagle insists that it "could have gone another way." But in a sense, troll culture didn't really hijack the revolutionary potential inherent in social media culture. Rather than ripping the fabric, troll culture astutely followed the seams and stitching to where they logically led.

The ideology of any social media platform makes it easy to misunderstand what one is doing as being highly individualized, and to forget that the platform is set up to enable and disable certain communicative maneuvers. As Nick Srnicek, a researcher of digital capitalism, has put it, the great commercial platforms may present themselves "as an empty vessel for market forces," but in truth they shape "the appearance of a market." The same is true for the great communication platforms. The troll represents a double exploitation of this state of affairs: He exploits the fact that the platform doesn't just passively reflect a "marketplace of ideas" (if there were such a thing) but rather shapes what kind of content can be transported. And he exploits the fact that the companies running the platform can't really acknowledge this fact.

It's not that certain platforms (ahem, Twitter.com) tend by some crazy fluke to be lousy with trolling, shit-posting, and abuse. They are set up to enable it. They live by engagement, and that means by exchange: not of information but of triggers. The troll plays the instrument the way it's meant to be played. And the instrument's creator is forced to pretend that the opposite is true. He has to adopt the hand-wringing stance that some Platonic ideal of communication animates the platform, standing beatifically and serenely behind the flat-earth videos, anti-Semitic memes, and call-out videos.

The troll understands this. He may think of himself as a kind of communicative guerrillero, finding "libtards" in their safe spaces and triggering them. But there's another aspect to trolling: the sense that it isn't so much sand in the gears of the machine as sand in the spirit of those gears. There is an Edgar Allan Poe story called "The Imp of the Perverse," which is Poe's description of the part of us that, when we peer into an abyss, fantasizes about what it would be like to fall into it; that, when we are pressed for time on a task, finds itself obsessed with every show on Netflix; that, when we engage in pleasantries, wonders what it would be like to withhold them. Such moments, Poe proposes, are not a matter of our individual psychology. "The speaker is aware that he displeases; he has every intention to please." But something else takes over, something objective, almost physical. There is something of that imp in every troll: If I don't post this, the troll thinks, someone else will step in and fulfill the exact same function. One way or the other, it will be posted.

And there is something of that imp in all of us. Have you ever looked at a rote, overly earnest conversation on social media and suddenly thought of the most absurd, digressive, inappropriate thing you could post? You might have chuckled at it, might have experienced a moment's temptation, but in most instances, you would never post it. It's almost as though the potential of trolling is out there, objectively if spectrally, even if you aren't the one who seizes it, even if no one does. Unlike you, using your real name in a conversation on Facebook, the troll is usually anonymous. So while Poe's imp is about moments when we are impelled toward acts of self-destruction, the troll provides all the destruction without all the self.

In gaming terms, trolling is an exploit. While they are

looking to trigger you emotionally, the trolls are triggered mechanistically, almost like an alarm. You tweet with a certain hashtag, share a particular article, are a particular gender, use a specific phrase, and there they are. The automatism of it, the lack of specificity in their attack, is part of the power play. It's the sense of compulsion encapsulated in the infamous phrase "well, actually": they literally can't help themselves. When the journalist Sarah Jeong joined *The New York Times*'s editorial board in the summer of 2018, right-wing trolls dug up some old tweets of hers and reposted them out of context. Since then, almost every single one of Jeong's tweets is responded to with variations of tweets calling her racist, claiming she hates white people, and so forth. As one troll put it in February 2019 (and I'm picking this example out of a large and very gross hat): "You should have been fired but since you weren't we are going to have to sentence you to life in the prison of Twitter trolls."

If there is something automatic about the way in which the same disproved canards attach to Jeong's tweets, it may well be because the replies are automated. But the more interesting fact about them is probably this: an aggrieved white guy who has set up an alert for when Sarah Jeong tweets and then huddles over his phone to make some claim about racism and *Roseanne* using jagged grammar and vertiginous logic is functionally indistinguishable from a bot having been set up to do the same thing. Call it a reverse Turing test. And this is part of the "sentence" the trolls have imposed on Jeong: the "prison of Twitter trolls" is made of people deliberately behaving like algorithms.

As Ralph Hartley, one of the pioneers of information theory in the 1920s, argued, the amount of information carried by a system of communication is a direct result of freedom of choice: a signal that by necessity *must* follow another signal can carry no new information; it is redundant. The troll is the ultimate sender of redundant messages. The imagination behind the act of trolling consists partly in thinking you're the Rebel Alliance sticking it to the power structure, and partly in thinking you're the Death Star. The sense that you are the ghost in the machine. You are the power structure, disembodied, deindividualized.

In her 1975 essay "Fascinating Fascism," Susan Sontag claimed that "fascist art glorifies surrender, it exalts mindlessness, it glamorizes death." Fascist aesthetics identified what fascism understood to be all-powerful forces in nature and society, then made proud common cause with those forces. These aesthetics identified with the aggressor. Sontag had in mind Freud's notion of the death drive—the idea that human aggression frequently flows from an unconscious desire to become inanimate, that there is pleasure to be had in ceasing to be a subject. Whenever we go online, we are faced with the objectivity of algorithms that we cannot understand. The troll gets to fancy himself the black box.

The Spanish fascists had the absurd rallying cry *Viva la muerte*, "Long live death." The troll follows a similar idea, destroying the self and any pretense of sending an actual message. We are often told that everything lives forever online. We warn young people against posting embarrassing pictures to their social media accounts. Victims of trolling like Sarah Jeong are finding that the opposite can also be true—if, that is, people fully divest from what they put online. The troll stops by, triggers you, and has moved on from whatever point he's just made by the time you actually manage to get offended by it. Trolls are like ghosts, and the only person left, feeling slightly embarrassed for having been caught up in the game, is you.

.5.

Desire

Spend enough time around any university and you'll come across certain clusters of smart people drawn to the intellectual life of the university without necessarily partaking in it. Their groups don't involve faculty, or if there are faculty in attendance, they seem confused and faintly embarrassed to be there. There are never any students at their meetings, a fact that the moderator will inevitably lament in a tone that leaves no doubt that it's the students' fault. The audience is made up of retired members of the community, people whose affiliation with the university extends to their having a gym card but not a library card, and people who have the general air of donors, even though they're never actually seen donating anything.

The preoccupations of these circles will vary from university to university, but they're inevitably things the institution is, according to the circle's members, too cowardly or small-minded to teach. The very fact that it's the same aging visiting scholars and retired local dentists chewing over the master's work week after week is taken as a sign of the iconoclasm of the work done here. There's a general undertone of pique to the proceedings. The fact that they have to meet here, in the alumni center, in the room behind the chapel, is the most visible symptom of an unconscionable disregard. The type of thinking these sorts of gatherings are drawn to is invariably bold and inevitably bogus. They are drawn to theories of everything that wind up explaining barely anything, that tend to become self-revealing rather than world-changing.

On Stanford's campus, one of these groups is the Girardians, followers of René Girard, a scholar of religion and literature who passed away in 2015. Girard was an unlikely evangelist for Silicon Valley. He was an academic writer, and not the most lucid one. He didn't teach courses on subjects budding techies would take a natural interest in, nor did his work touch on technology very much. Moreover, he was most famous in his native France, where he became a member of the Académie Française in 2005, won prestigious prizes, and was a noted public intellectual.

His books, like *Violence and the Sacred* (1972) and *The Scapegoat* (1982), had a broad impact across the academy—in religious as well as literary studies, in departments of anthropology and philosophy. But this impact was concentrated largely on university campuses and in Catholic seminaries. Girard therefore comes to matter to our story for primarily geographic reasons: he became a bit player in the intellectual history of Silicon Valley when he accepted a professorship in the Department of Comparative Literature at Stanford in 1981. He would stay in Palo Alto for the rest of his life.

The students that Girard, a magnetic lecturer and far-ranging thinker, inspired there were part of the generation that made Silicon Valley into what it is today. Some of them, including and above all Peter Thiel, became extremely successful and used some of their wealth to spread the gospel of Girard. As Thiel has described, when he arrived at Stanford in 1985, "it was one of these ideas that was starting to percolate in the underground that there was this very interesting professor with a different account from the world." And while Thiel doesn't regard higher education particularly well, he seems to have only happy memories of Girard. He's expressed his belief that "when the history of the twentieth century is written circa 2100, he'll be seen as truly one of the great intellectuals."

The Thiel Foundation, set up in 2006, has taken an active role in disseminating Girard's "mimetic theory"—it is one of the foundation's three central tasks, along with the Thiel Fellowships and an incubator program for small companies. The Imitatio group within the foundation funds book series, periodicals, and conferences. Thanks to the foundation's money, the Girardians' reach is far. They are well connected within Stanford's fabulously wealthy Hoover Institution. More recently, the Imitatio crew provided intellectual cover and manpower for Donald Trump's transition team—suddenly, people you'd see around Stanford's campus trying to put together panels to discuss Girard's work seemed to be taking up offices in Trump Tower. A strange trajectory for any academic theory, let alone one in the humanities.

So what, exactly, did Girard teach? Be prepared to be further mystified, because although what follows is not at all uninteresting, the path from Girard to the Thiel Foundation to Trump Tower is not exactly a straight line. Girard believed he had discovered that all human desire is mimetic—anything you desire is a mirror of another person's desire for that same thing. Our desires are not ours;

they are born from neither our autonomous whims nor any feature of the desired object. Girard calls the stories we tell ourselves about our desires, and how they come from either our objects or ourselves, the "romantic lie." All our desires come out of a network of copied desires—we like what others like. Perhaps it's not entirely surprising that someone drawn to this theory saw value in Facebook when Mark Zuckerberg first made his pitch.

Since we necessarily desire the same objects as other people, conflicts over those objects are not so much unfortunate accidents as inherent in the nature of desire itself. In any society, mimetic desire thus creates constant competition and conflict. But every society also finds a huge number of ways to continually displace onto new victims the violence generated by mimetic desire. According to Girard, the primary way in which society does this is the scapegoat mechanism: the omnipresent mimetic rivalry gets displaced on a purely innocent object—a sacrificial lamb. Most ritual and culture, according to Girard, consists of mechanisms by which this displacement is accomplished. Only in rare instances is this endless victimization made explicit, and even rarer are cases where the mechanism of displacement reveals itself. Until, that is, the crucifixion of Christ.

In God's offering up his own son to die as a scapegoat, the dynamic becomes spectacularly evident, and, in a way, backfires. What's revealed, Girard thinks, are the workings of mimetic desire, and what they make human beings do. And the salvation that revelation promises consists primarily of self-knowledge: if we understand the structure of our desire and what makes that structure so dangerous, we can learn to overcome it. You can see what might appeal to theologians and anthropologists about this theory. It's much harder to imagine what might have appealed to Stanford undergraduates with a pronounced interest in tech.

The first thing that may have attracted them: mimetic theory was boldly syncretic. Even among the porous disciplinary boundaries that have long defined Stanford, Girard's thought ranged widely. Thiel calls him one of the "last great generalists who is really interested in everything." Girard spoke to the energy of boldly jumping across established or traditional boundaries—between fields of study, between historical periods, between disciplines. And he suggested that the university was perhaps no longer the place for such boldness. Little wonder that a group of innovators, who sensed that in order to succeed they'd need to transcend all manner of boundaries that tradition had placed on them, were drawn to Girard's big story.

Another idea Thiel could have gotten from Girard, but probably didn't have to, was that people are basically sheep. For Thiel, mimetic theory revealed and explained "how disturbingly herdlike people become in so many different contexts"—something he thinks mimetic theory helped him break out of and manipulate at the same time. That people are herdlike may not strike you as a particularly original point. But by drawing this insight from a fairly niche theory rather than from, say, behavioral psychology, Thiel could reframe, as he did in a 2009 interview, what is arguably a cliché as rather "knowledge that is generally suppressed and hidden." In other words, Girard provided for

Thiel a mystical knowledge that was, when stripped of its rarefied vocabulary and references, really not that different from the common sense of his particular milieu.

But there was a political dimension as well to Thiel's embrace of Girard. By the 1980s, the academy at large had abandoned the big narratives, and in 1987, Stanford, under pressure from activist groups and even from the Reverend Jesse Jackson, decided to get rid of its Western Civilization course sequence. People like Thiel found in Girard a traditional reader of the old European-centered canon—one, moreover, who could give them, perhaps without meaning to, a vocabulary to think through their particular moment on a university campus. Girard warned of endless cycles of violence, where persecution could be "pursued in the name of anti-persecution." Thiel wrote an entire book about the racial politics of Stanford, *The Diversity Myth: Multiculturalism and Political Intolerance on Campus* (1995), in which he and his coauthor (and later fellow PayPal mafioso), David O. Sacks, lamented what they described as groupthink and a persecution of conservative students.

But Girard's oeuvre presented the good old canon with a twist—all the established authors are there and still great, but they are great for an entirely new, previously unglimpsed reason. In *The Diversity Myth*, Thiel argued that multiculturalism, "instead of representing an advance on the Western religious and cultural tradition," was "its perversion." Girard reaffirmed the importance of that cultural tradition while at the same time disrupting it.

There is an odd tension in the concept of "disruption," and you can sense it here: disruption acts as though it thoroughly disrespects whatever existed previously, but in truth it often seeks to simply rearrange whatever exists. It is possessed of a deep fealty to whatever is already given. It seeks to make it more efficient, more exciting, more *something*, but it never wants to dispense altogether with what's out there. This is why its gestures are always radical but its effects never really upset the apple cart: Uber claims to have "revolutionized" the experience of hailing a cab, but really that experience has stayed largely the same. What it managed to get rid of were steady jobs, unions, and anyone other than Uber's making money on the whole enterprise.

Girard is a disrupter of tradition in exactly this mold: whatever thinkers or poets you thought were important before you read Girard, you will still think they are important after. If you thought dead white men were pretty much all you needed to read, you'll still think so after reading Girard. But he will have taught you entirely new reasons why they're important. Girard's philosophy was, in other words, disruptive in precisely the way that Silicon Valley likes: "bombastic redescription of orthodoxy," as the philosopher Daniel Dennett once put it.

While Girard's thought managed to be appealingly far-ranging, it was at the same time monomaniacal: rather than abandon himself eclectically to this field or that, this idea or that, he was always in search of a kind of master code, one that unified, according to him, a vast corpus of literary works, religious practices, human mythology, societal phenomena, and historical events. Behind *The Epic of Gilgamesh* and Proust's *In Search of Lost Time*, behind advertising and Dostoyevsky, lay—if you knew how to look—

the machinations of mimetic desire. Sure, you sort of had to squint to make it work, but mimetic theory provided a kind of elegant reduction of an otherwise baffling range of phenomena.

It is perhaps unsurprising that adolescents and nerds, two groups not known for their love of social cues, might find something to like in an anthropology that pureed the bewildering variety across human society and history into easily digestible Soylent. Once you have figured out that all desire is mimetic, you see examples everywhere. Thiel himself pointed out in an interview that mimetic theory allows you to say, "This is really what's happening in this moment." Thanks to mimetic theory, you always know better than the people around you; and thanks to mimetic theory, you have a useful dispensation from the need to actually look at anything very closely.

Believing Girard's claims requires a very specific kind of squinting. His colleague Joshua Landy once pointedly asked just what sort of fact mimetic desire is supposed to be. If Girard's claim were that literally all desires are mimetic, this would seem to be demonstrably wrong: What about desires that mix the necessary (meaning, features of the object) with the merely pleasing (meaning, features we might project onto them)? Wouldn't there have to be a first desire that all other desires then mimic? Would this first desire not be nonmimetic? How do we decide the medium from whom we take our desire? Wouldn't deciding this require autonomy?

If, on the other hand, Girard's claim were that *a lot* of desire is mimetic, then we'd have to ask why we need a theory to assert a truism. The idea that there are mimetic desires is so obvious that having a theory about it is like having a theory that some cats are mean. Sure, it's true, but is it worth a spot in the Académie Française?

What Landy does not say: this strange space, between a pretend universality and a far more modest claim that is so self-evident as to be a cliché, is where a lot of Silicon Valley's global pronouncements make their home—the pronouncements about what "mankind" has always wanted, what "everyone" needs, and so forth. And in each case, it seems to be plain bad sportsmanship to poke at the claim's supposed universality; it's more fun to play along. The kind of faith Girard required of his readers, in other words, was the same kind of faith a lot of tech evangelists have become accustomed to asking of their audience. And why, after all, shouldn't they? Wouldn't it just be so much simpler, so much more elegant, if claims such as these were really *universally* true? If people had always desired X, or all Y was actually Z? Statements of this nature are selling themselves as "user experience" more than as truth claims.

These are the argumentative gambits used in books by Malcolm Gladwell and Jonah Lehrer, in TED Talks and pitch meetings. Statements that claim that we "tend to assume X," when in fact a brief reflection would tell us that no, we don't tend to assume anything as stupid as X. Statements that blow up some study's perfectly plausible finding to a generalization that would give the study's author a heart attack. Statements that repackage trite wisdom in verbiage meant to suggest that it is utterly counterintuitive.

Girard's claims are far more interesting than those of Silicon Valley. But the appeal they hold for a certain kind of thinker may well depend on a very similar cognitive operation. After all, the flimsiness of these gambits is part of their appeal: we're being invited to play along, and if we don't, we risk coming across as scolds. Wouldn't it just be so much more pleasing and elegant if this were true, if that claim were plausible, if that conclusion truly were counterintuitive?

Ultimately, then, Girard's success may tell us something about how *faith* functions in Silicon Valley. Of course, it's not fair to compare religious faith to the glib stock the very smart people in the Valley seem to put in very dumb ideas. But more than most industries, tech companies seem to run on tropes and rituals that remind you of a tent revival: the mantra-like phrases, the messianic gurus, the cult of genius that barely manages to cover up its religious dimensions.

It is quite possible that Girard never intended his philosophy to be understood as a philosophical anthropology— that is to say, a picture of what human beings are like. Instead, he may have intended it as theology: a picture of the world in codependence with God. It certainly makes more sense as the latter, and it's surely not an accident that some of Girard's most sensitive readers have been priests.

But where Silicon Valley is concerned, that may well be a feature rather than a bug. Is it possible that the story here is not that a bunch of techies misunderstand what philosophy is, but instead that they intuit something that was not, in fact, offered as philosophy? That Thiel recognizes in Girard's claim precisely the kind of catechism of faith that Silicon Valley has built so much of its success on? That it allows tech CEOs to give substance to their sacerdotal allures?

In a 2009 interview with Daniel Lance from Thiel's own institute, Thiel was asked what lessons he drew from Girard in running his businesses. His answer is revealing. He credits mimetic theory with helping him think "about how to avoid conflict within a business," to reduce "counterproductive" internal disagreements. What makes that answer fascinating is that Thiel thinks mimetic theory, which, remember, claims that conflict between mirroring desires is pretty much inevitable, could actually tell us how to avoid that conflict. There's no Jesus in this story to make visible the bad effects of mimetic desire. But there are smart young people banding together to seed startups. Tech will set us free.

Or perhaps it's the other way around: as the journalist Geoff Shullenberger suggested, Thiel may have viewed sacrificial religion as a technology. Thiel is fond of defining technology as "doing more with less." Is the scapegoat mechanism perhaps one such way of doing more with less? Or is the overcoming of this mechanism? It is hard not to be struck by the fact that the company Thiel made most of his money from, Facebook, is all about the algorithmic desire for incessant reciprocal rating and awarding of status. But perhaps more striking is that Thiel seems to think that the same mechanisms will operate on the other side of the algorithm—among the coders and designers, the CEOs and investors.

There is an entire worldview contained in that idea. A worldview in which companies falter not on competition, being outmaneuvered, or growing too slowly or quickly but on the interpersonal conflicts between a bunch of alpha males who all want identical things. A worldview in which these conflicts can be avoided if the men involved are made to realize just how similar they really are. Thiel's world, even when it doesn't seek to send literal artificial islands into international waters in order to get away from human society and all the messes it makes, is insular, extremely conflict-averse, and allergic to difference. Of course, that is not exactly a limitation when it comes to picking investments in an industry where companies run by a bunch of white boys from the same Stanford frat can make billions or fall apart depending on how well the boys get along. This situation might constitute the one social formation in which Girard's theory holds 100 percent true.

In a 2012 seminar at Stanford, some ideas from which ended up in his 2014 book, *Zero to One*, Thiel at several points came close to suggesting that the CEO of a company may fall victim to scapegoating mechanisms just like the ones that felled Jesus Christ. This particular idea didn't make it into *Zero to One*, though it shows up in the class notes taken by his coauthor, Blake Masters. But one need only listen to Thiel when he believes he is defending himself against attacks—especially when justifying his Ahab-like vendetta against the now-defunct news and commentary site Gawker—to hear echoes of this worldview. In interviews from 2016, Thiel repeatedly describes Gawker as a bully and bemoans the experiences of the many, many rich and famous people it went after, calling them its victims. Unsurprisingly, ideas that allow the hyperpowerful to cast themselves as victims are popular in Silicon Valley. Girard's may well be only the most philosophically ambitious and historically literate version.

We have encountered the idea of the rich and powerful being the true victims before. For Thiel, mimetic desire is something we can achieve mastery over in ourselves; and since others won't be quite as good at such mastery, or sufficiently aware to achieve it, our self-knowledge puts us in a position to manipulate others. There are clear echoes of Ayn Rand in this version of Girard, but also far more pedestrian echoes of the motivational guru Tony Robbins: it reimagines as a marketing trick the human being's status as a fallen creature. We can be saved, then turn around and monetize other people's sinfulness.

So it isn't just that Girard's followers in Silicon Valley get to imagine themselves as keepers of an esoteric knowledge few others possess. They also believe this knowledge gives them the ability to become leaders of others. It should be clear why tech people and academics—two groups given to delusions of this type—might be particularly drawn to mimetic theory.

For all the features of Girard's theory that Silicon Valley has intuitively grasped and glommed on to, there are others that seem to have conveniently disappeared over the short trip from Jane Stanford Way to the VC firms on Sand Hill Road. For one thing, Girard's theory is relentlessly pessimistic. After all, for Girard, Christ did not die redeeming us but rather making visible the fundamental awfulness of our predicament. Girard at times sounds like he thinks our self-knowledge will, to some extent, free us from mimetic desire, but he's not altogether sanguine on that score.

Listen to Peter Thiel talk about the same questions—and he talks about them surprisingly frequently—and you'll hear a totally different version of Girard. It is one that is far more optimistic, and optimistic in a way that Girard's readers in the seminaries might see as Christian, but that has likely taken a few detours from its origin. Girard seems genuinely allergic to human community. Given the violence he sees at its center, it could hardly be otherwise. He puts his hope for redemption in self-knowledge.

Thiel shares Girard's disgust for society, for the public, for politics, but he thinks redemption can come from a well-managed, small company of like-minded individuals. It's highly dubious that Girard would have thought that the PayPal mafia was the solution to mimetic desire. Thiel likes the PayPal mafia so much he renders it sacred.

Girard's ideas are another flyby between tech and the academy. The Girardians may lament the marginal status of his theories within the academy; even Thiel may lament it. But secretly, or not so secretly, that marginality is what draws a man like Thiel to Girard. For in Girard you get your own intuitions repackaged as esoteric knowledge. You get a feeling of oppositionality while remaining at the center of things. You get to feel like a victim while having all the power. And this, as we'll see, may be the most secret of Silicon Valley's secret desires.

.6.

Disruption

"Disruption" is one of those concepts that unify in an almost wondrous way the stuff of dry economics lectures and our everyday experience. Because I am not an economist, I can't draw the requisite graphs for you. But because I am someone who recently moved houses, I can describe to you the feeling of holding an old TI-83 graphing calculator in my hands. I can describe to you how it felt to send my copy of the *Encyclopedia Britannica* to Goodwill: not exactly sad, but melancholy at how I didn't feel sad. Thanks to technology, thanks in particular to the technology introduced by Silicon Valley, this is a feeling we're becoming more and more familiar with: some objects have fallen so thoroughly out of our lives that we cannot even muster the energy to miss them.

The concept of disruption allows companies, the press, or simply individuals working in an office in Los Gatos, California, or behind the desk of a video store, to articulate questions of continuity and discontinuity. But neither those who argue for continuity nor those in favor of discontinuity are disinterested parties—everyone has a stake in these things. One ought to be skeptical of unsubstantiated claims of something's being totally new and not following the hitherto established rules (of business, of politics, of common sense), just as one is skeptical of claims that something which really does feel and look unprecedented is simply a continuation of the status quo.

Characteristically, both types of claims often unite the gloomiest of doomsayers with the giddiest of cheerleaders. Take, for example, the idea that reading books on e-readers represents a totally different kind of reading. I have a lot of colleagues who are very invested in this idea, and they almost all wield it as a warning: Come back to our kind of reading, they say, put down that Kindle, or else you'll be stupider than people who just leaf through an object they picked up at Barnes & Noble. However, their central premise agrees with that of Amazon and others: even though you do many of the same things when you pick up a book on your Kindle or a store-bought hardcover, it's actually totally different. The disruption warning coming from my colleagues is pretty much identical to the tech world's advertising pitch for the Kindle.

Conversely, the claim that something seemingly disruptive is, in truth, just part of a bigger continuity can itself be either critical or deeply conservative. It comes from an intuition that is shared by those who want to deflate the tech industry's high-minded blather about itself and those who are paid to argue that Amazon should not be regulated any more than your friendly neighborhood bookseller. To be clear: all of these answers are absolutely right some of the time. Certain things about the tech industry are unprecedented (the tech, for one); others are business as usual (the industry). But how the public, the press, and politicians respond to both the tech and its industry depends on a sense of what our current categories are able to capture, and what they need to be adjusted to be able to capture. Disruption is one way that allows people to do both.

But the concept of disruption also tells a more covert and fundamental story about continuity and discontinuity, and it concerns capitalism. Are the changes the tech industry brings, or claims to bring, fundamental transformations of how capitalism functions, or are they an extension, perhaps a bit less varnished, of how it has always functioned? You can see why different parties would have a lot at stake in the answer to this question: it determines what regulatory oversight is necessary or desirable, what role the government or unions should play in a new industry like tech, and even how the industry and its titans ought to be discussed.

I have to include myself in this. I confess to being very leery of claims of disruption, but then again, I'm in a profession that pretty much depends on the idea that the past matters a lot and that messing with it in any meaningful sense entails spending a lot of time studying it. As Mandy Rice-Davies put it when she was told that the politician Lord Astor denied having an affair with her: "Well, he would, wouldn't he?" And I would argue that stewardship of the past is more important than riding roughshod over it, wouldn't I?

At the same time, I think it is also true that some of the rhetoric of disruption depends on actively misunderstanding and misrepresenting the past. We can call this the infomercial effect. You don't see quite so many of them today, but they were once ubiquitous, and they'd follow the same template: "Don't you hate it when," they'd ask, and name an extremely minor problem with some mundane task you honestly couldn't say you'd ever encountered. Then they'd offer their revolutionary solution to the problem they had just invented. The infomercial deliberately misinterpreted whatever it was seeking to disrupt. One of the internet age's greatest works of collective satire may be the 5,875 and counting Amazon reviews for the Hutzler 571 banana slicer, which mock the mania for buzzy solutions in search of a problem.

The reason infomercials use this template is that it taps into a pretty pervasive sense of boredom. We get excited when things are shaken up, when the big and powerful are taken down a peg. One testament to this is the notion that the sheer size of an industry makes it ripe for disruption. Not that it is inefficient, or doesn't do its job well. Just that it is big. The point here is to say that a startup might be able to make a lot of money. But the notion actually has not-so-subtle delegitimizing notes: the very fact that X, Y, or Z is a multibillion-dollar company makes it a little suspicious.

Is it an accident that this formula is frequently deployed when the tech media are at their most credulous? There is joy in seeing "the system" shaken up, old hierarchies upended, Goliaths being felled by Davids. In a long interview with *Vanity Fair*, the Napster creator and devil on Mark Zuckerberg's shoulder Sean Parker once described himself as "an archetypal Loki character"— disruption is a prankster god, and who doesn't love those? Disruption plays to our impatience with structures and situations that seem to coast on habit and inertia, and it plays to the press's excitement about underdogs, rebels, outsiders. If you look back at coverage of Theranos, up until the fateful John Carreyrou story in *The Wall Street Journal* that brought the company down, you'll find that few journalists really bothered to ask whether or not Theranos could do what it claimed to be able to do—they asked instead what would happen if it could. Disruption is high drama. The notion that "things work the way they work because there's a certain logic to them" is not.

Disruption has become a way to tell a story about the meaning of both discontinuity and continuity. The latter part is often overlooked. Because the way the term is used today really implies that whatever continuity is being disrupted *deserved* to be disrupted. The very fact of X having been in charge is taken as evidence that X ought no longer to be in charge. Even if X is a doctor telling you to vaccinate your kid against measles.

As the management professor Joshua Gans has put it, disruption's opposite is companies or people failing by doing what they've always done. When we speak of disruption, we are usually thinking about the perils of continuity; we express the sense that continuity works fine until it doesn't. To some extent, the sense that stasis is dangerous, and puts us at risk of falling behind, is characteristic of modernity—not a specific time period so much as the condition of being modern, living in a modern age. As the poet Charles Baudelaire wrote when the world around him was modernizing at a breakneck pace, "The form of a city / changes faster, alas, than a mortal's heart." Keep living the way you're living, and soon enough you'll find yourself living in the past.

More specifically, though, disruption resonates well with our experience of capitalism—for if Baudelaire was shocked that he could outlive the form of his city, he would have been doubly shocked to measure his life span against that of the average corporation today. Think of all the companies and products you remember treating as permanent, inextricable fixtures of your everyday life, that nevertheless slid right out and disappeared over time. Recall, if you're the right age, the act of respooling a cassette tape with your pinkie finger, or the phrase "Be kind, please rewind." Or, for a slightly younger generation, the whistles of a dial-up modem or the mastication of a floppy disk drive.

Disruption tells a story of how things that work hard to appear eternal nevertheless come to be short-lived. Disruption looks for the foreshocks within stability. At the same time, we probably shouldn't discount that sense of stability altogether. Is it purely illusory? Or does it get at something important about these gestures, actions, and objects that are reiterated in and integrated into the fabric of our everyday life? On the one hand, you may be unable to remember the last visit you made to a Blockbuster. On the other, you probably remember the pervading sense of shitty permanence that Blockbuster stores projected. At least when it comes to the ordering of our experience of capitalism, it would seem, stability and impermanence are equally valid: nothing lasts forever, but everything lives by pretending it will.

The idea of disruption has a particularly strange genealogy. Its oldest ancestors are probably Karl Marx and Friedrich Engels, who wrote in *The Communist Manifesto* (1848) that the modern capitalist world is characterized by "constant revolutionizing of production, uninterrupted disturbance of all social conditions," so that, as they put it, "all that is solid melts into air." Whereas the premodern world was defined by a few stable certainties and centuries-old tradition, and governed by ancient habits of thought, in modernity all fixed relations "are swept away, all new-formed ones become antiquated before they can ossify." You can sense their giddiness, even though the situation they describe is disorienting and nightmarish. And yet they are giddy, because they feel that this accelerating cycle of constant destruction and replacement ultimately destroys itself.

This idea made its way from *The Communist Manifesto* into business jargon by way of the Austrian economist Joseph Schumpeter (1883–1950), who, in a 1942 book, coined the phrase "creative destruction." Although hardly a communist himself, Schumpeter derived the term from Marx and intended it to be descriptive rather than affirmative. Born in Austria, Schumpeter was steeped in both Marxian economics and the work of classical liberal economists like Ludwig von Mises. He became one of the great analysts of the business cycle, but also of its social ramifications. In 1932 he became a professor at Harvard. A few of the shorter works he published in the United States give an idea of his overall thinking: in 1928 he gave a talk titled "The Instability of Capitalism," and in 1949 he gave a cautionary lecture called "The March into Socialism" at the meeting of the American Economic Association. Schumpeter thought that capitalism would gradually lead to some kind of state socialism, a fact he didn't exactly welcome but thought inevitable.

The instability of capitalism and the inevitability of socialism are two ideas one rarely hears mentioned today in connection with disruption. If anything, disruption seems to lean in the direction of *more* capitalism, of cast-off fetters and a more untrammeled expression of market forces. But it's significant that this theory was first developed in dialogue with a philosopher who was trying to show that the capitalist mode of production made a revolution inevitable. Schumpeter agreed with Marx on two important points: that the ever-increasing efficiency of capitalist exploitation inevitably decreases the rate of profit, and that decreased rate of profit leads to monopolies.

Marx thought that the falling rate of profit doomed capitalism to exploit labor ever more harshly (thus setting the stage for revolution). Schumpeter countered with the idea of creative destruction: if markets were uniform over time, Marx might well have been proven correct, but this turns out not to be the case: "The fundamental impulse that sets and keeps the capitalist engine in motion comes from the new consumers' goods, the new methods of production or transportation, the new markets, the new forms of industrial organization that capitalist enterprise creates." Capitalism's "creative destruction" of everything solid in the market, its tendency to shake up and redefine its markets, is the thing that actually accounts for its continuity. Yesterday's monopolist is suddenly one competitor among many, and often enough goes under entirely. The cycle begins anew.

It would have been easy enough for Schumpeter to argue that, in this way, creative destruction would ensure capitalism's long-term viability. But interestingly, in his 1942 magnum opus, *Capitalism, Socialism and Democracy*, Schumpeter argues just the opposite. It's not necessarily a good thing that capitalism tends toward oligopolies that then have to be disrupted and destroyed by outside challengers; it is simply how he (following Marx) thought capitalism worked. Part two of *Capitalism, Socialism and Democracy* is titled "Can Capitalism Survive?," and Schumpeter comes down on the side of no. After all, the constant destruction, however generative it may be from a bird's-eye view, will ultimately prompt attempts to regulate capitalism. While creative destruction is viable economically, the experience of it is too disorienting politically to allow capitalism to survive long-term.

In a way, the concept of creative destruction sublimates the concept of revolution. Because creative destruction resets the playing field, it forestalls the processes Marx had predicted. Sure, capital tends toward monopolization, but then someone comes in from the outside and pulls the rug out from under the monopolist. On the other hand, for Schumpeter the process Marx had (correctly) forecast resulted in creative destruction rather than revolution. If Marx had been right, and greater and greater monopolization led inevitably to a declining rate of profits and therefore to lower wages, then we would indeed expect capitalism to lead to a revolution. Schumpeter thought Marx was wrong and that creative destruction would forestall both the drive toward monopolization and the declining profit rate. But in the end, creative destruction also makes capitalism unsustainable: gradually and peacefully (through elections and legislative action), capitalism will yield to some form of socialism.

Most of the discourse around disruption clearly draws on the idea of creative destruction, but it shifts it in important respects. Most centrally, it doesn't seem to suggest that the ever-intensifying rapids of creative destruction will eventually lead to the placid waters of a new stability, that hypercapitalism almost inevitably pushes us toward something beyond capitalism. Instead, disruption seems to suggest that the rapids are all there is and can be—we might as well strap in for the ride. Often enough, talk of disruption is a theodicy of hypercapitalism. Disruption is newness for people who are scared of genuine newness. Revolution for people who don't stand to gain anything from revolution.

The idea that modern capitalism generates an ever-accelerating rate of transformation, there is no endpoint, and the smartest thing to do is to lean into that rate of transformation, is called accelerationism. As Nick Land—who went from cofounding the Cybernetic Culture Research Unit at Warwick University, one of the more ambitious attempts to use French theory to think through the challenges posed by cyberculture, to becoming a fixture of the so-called Dark Enlightenment—framed the problem, "Thinking takes time, and accelerationism suggests we're running out of time to think that through." Accelerationism advocates a surrender to the forces of acceleration instead, jumping into the river even as we can hear the roar of the waterfall.

The famous futurologist Ray Kurzweil has put forth a similar idea: our predictions about the future are by necessity built out of linear extrapolations from past trends. But exponential change will often *appear* linear in the short term. The accelerationist humility, which Land adapts from the German philosopher Martin Heidegger, is an extreme form of something that is always part of the idea of disruption. We need to surrender to certain transformations; we need to let things die and embrace things that may at first seem uncomfortable or even unpleasant. We need to take a leap of faith, give in to the sense that certain developments are the beginnings of things that our current categories cannot fully map out. Clinging to our established categories, pieties, and preferences will prove counterproductive, perhaps even actively destructive.

Accelerationists largely believe that the processes of creative destruction inherent in the capitalist mode of production will inevitably lead to a transcendence of modern capitalism. But they differ on what that transcendence will look like: Will it mean a withering away of the state as technological and social development finally put the lie to any government attempt to constrain them? Will it mean an implosion of capitalism itself and its replacement by something more humane and less convulsive? Or will it mean an overcoming of the human, as man and machine hurtle toward a point of indistinction—for instance, in what Ray Kurzweil has called the singularity?

There is a weak messianism inherent in this idea. It trembles with the sense that we are accelerating toward a kind of rapture, toward a future that may now be glimpsed through a glass darkly, if at all, but will soon become bright as day. But as messianisms go, it's usually fairly weak: Kurzweil is one of the few thinkers who commits to the idea that you can't tell this story without guessing where the story might end. And his idea of the singularity is deliberately monumental: a galaxy-engulfing hive mind that no longer knows the outside, a place where the distinction between humans and the technology they use has completely withered away and we dwell in the synaptic pathways of the universe amid wonder and glory forever.

It's batshit, but it's deliberately batshit. Unless you go for broke, Kurzweil thinks, you're bound to miss the exponential changes imagined by accelerationism. Most advocates of disruption don't have that forthrightness. Their faith in disruption draws on a similar faith in a future that's radically different, but they don't deign to describe it in too much detail. Ironically, as much as disruption functions as a welcome corrective to systems whose legitimacy seems to rely mostly on the lazy halo of long tradition, disruption itself draws its legitimacy from the dim first embers of a never-actually-glimpsed future.

The most obvious shift that has occurred in the use of the term "creative destruction" is that it now has an exculpatory, at times even celebratory, side. The famous mantra "Move fast and break things" goes well beyond a surrender to the inevitability of acceleration, instead making acceleration an ethical imperative. If the Latins said that the world "wants to be deceived," tech seems to think that it wants to be accelerated. Schumpeter wasn't altogether horrified by creative destruction, but he thought it was as much of a problem as it was a functional rule for how capitalism operates. By the 1990s, "creative destruction" had become an exonerating byword, used typically when someone wanted to push back against government regulation or public opprobrium for certain business practices. Evangelists of downsizing and hostile takeovers, such as the business professors Richard Nolan and David Croson, relied on the term.

While "creative destruction" is a deeply ambivalent phrase, the word "disruption" is frequently positioned as something to be explicitly celebrated. It becomes something to be taught and striven for. And where Schumpeter's perspective of the business cycle assumes a kind of Olympian view from above, disruption puts us in the trenches, presumably on the side of the attacker rather than the stalwart. While creative destruction was neutral on whether whatever was getting creatively destroyed deserved it, anything that is getting disrupted had it coming.

But there is a less obvious shift in usage, especially when we turn specifically to contemporary thinking about disruption. Schumpeter proposed creative destruction as a concept that applies to the business cycle. Companies dominate the market, are challenged by other companies that operate entirely differently, and are displaced. But today's rhetoric of disruption frequently applies to things other than companies. This is why people like Peter Thiel are so intent on claiming that higher education, say, or health care as a whole, or government are oligopolies or even monopolies. Schumpeter almost certainly would have looked at Blockbuster's gradual defeat by Netflix—a rival it never saw coming, a rival that when threatened it didn't take seriously and even refused to buy when given the chance—as a textbook case of creative destruction. But is the same true for your local travel agency, record store, and pharmacist? Is it true of the postal service or the regional bus company? Disruption is a concept that draws combatants into an arena they had no idea they were entering.

The rhetoric of disruption frequently creates solidity, stability, and uniformity where they didn't exist. Just as kvetching over political correctness often requires the invention of the restrictions and pieties which it sees itself as engaged in a titanic struggle against, so the disrupter portrays even the most staid cottage industry as a Death Star against which its plucky rebels have to do battle. Misperceiving, misunderstanding, or simply ignoring the industry one is seeking to disrupt seems, if not necessary, then at least no impediment to disrupting it. The world is out there, stupid and driven by habits. You just graduated from college and have had a credit card for three years. You're still on your parents' car insurance. Would the world in that situation not seem like one large opportunity for disruption?

Friedrich Nietzsche once wrote that "forgetfulness is a property of all action." If I could clearly see what everyone had done before me and what the consequences were, I would never act. To act decisively, Nietzsche proposed, requires a moment of egocentrism, "drawing a limited horizon round one's self," the power to be "super-historical." Disruption is premised on creative amnesia, on a productive or at least profitable disregard for details. Sometimes what comes out at the other end is a Tesla Model 3. Sometimes it's a Hutzler 571 banana slicer. The way the concept is used today is deeply suspicious of any cumulative force of progress. This despite the fact that while stories of gradual progress aren't as exciting as stories of people just flipping the game board, they actually end up describing the world we live in fairly well.

Disruption depends on regarding people as participating in the business cycle who insist that they're doing no such thing—another aspect of creative destruction that actually retains a lot of the idea's Marxist DNA. And it depends on an extension of the sense in which the terms "monopoly" or "oligopoly" can be applied. Did big taxi companies once dominate personal transportation, or did thousands of individual cabbies who were barely making ends meet? Did Yelp disrupt the oligopoly of people having an opinion? The term "disruption" makes a monolith of the particulars of the everyday, a leviathan out of structures and organizations that are old, have grown up organically, and are therefore pretty scattered and decentralized.

Think about the peculiar alchemy involved in talking about how Google disrupted the media landscape: suddenly the hundred-billion-dollar company is a scrappy underdog and a magazine with forty employees is a Big Bad Monopolist. The problem of scale is central to the tech industry more generally. We approach the economy with a certain sense of dimension. We know what the iconography of economic power looks like. It's pretty central to the success of the tech industry that it confuses that sense of dimension and refuses the iconography.

The final distortion the rhetoric of disruption introduces

concerns where society and the state lend their support. For Schumpeter, creative destruction comes from challengers who are able to spontaneously expand or change the playing field. But what happens when disruption itself becomes institutionalized? Today's plucky rebels are funded by billionaires, can go into massive debt if they need to, are supported by regulatory bodies they or their business school buddies have long ago captured, and are encouraged in their attacks by people who have wanted to get rid of unions and regulation all along. They are outsiders in only a very limited sense, or, not to put too fine a point on it, about as much as the horse was a victory gift to Troy.

And while it's hard to look at a company like Blockbuster and cheer it on in thinking that the market it found would remain uniform forever, it's also strange to look at companies like Uber and cheer them on in thinking that government regulation will eventually need to adjust to support their business model. For the upshot of the disrupter's super-historical impulse is the expectation that, rather than your idea conforming to the world in some manner, the world ought to accommodate the sheer genius of your idea.

When *Mad Money*'s Jim Cramer had Elizabeth Holmes on his show after the allegations against Theranos became public, she repeated a Jobs-ism (an infamous free-floating quote, variants of which have been ascribed to everyone from Mahatma Gandhi to Arthur Schopenhauer): "First they think you're crazy, then they fight you, and then all of a sudden you change the world." When challenged, Holmes retreated into a kind of received wisdom, but that wisdom seems to have been gleaned largely from dorm room motivational prints. Even so, there's a lot going on in that sentence.

Holmes was characteristically vague about who "they" were, but from the context, it seems likely that the naysayers were the Food and Drug Administration, the Centers for Medicare and Medicaid Services, and the Securities and Exchange Commission. So really she wasn't saying that Theranos's fictional tech was going to change the world; she was expecting the world to make Theranos's fictional tech real. Not that Theranos would be vindicated, but that the regulatory environment would have to warp to accommodate Theranos's way of doing business. She was blaming regulatory oversight for what that regulatory oversight found, for the FDA's craven insistence that technology should do what you claimed it did and that people should not be told they have diseases they don't actually have.

Her hope wasn't as crazy as it may sound; this was, after all, how it had worked in many other fields. Tech hasn't so much changed the rules as it has captured the norms by which the field is governed. And "disruption" probably refers to this disruption of our judgments and categories as well. But only the disrupter has this privilege. Anytime disruptees suggest that they might like to have the world adjusted to ensure their survival, they're told this is a sign of their weakness and resistance to change. This double standard applies to another Silicon Valley mantra as well: Do you want to "fail better" and "fail fast"? Well, whether you get to, and how your failure is interpreted, depends a great deal on who you are.

.7.

Failure

Silicon Valley thinks it has failure figured out. A tolerance for things not going quite right is baked into the tech industry—its love of dropouts being Exhibit A. This can be inspiring to see, but it can also be frustrating. People take jobs and lose them, then go on to new jobs; people create products no one likes, then go on to create other products—that's refreshing. People back companies that get investigated by the SEC, then go on to back other companies; they can even lie on behalf of a company like Theranos without much of a taint—that's perhaps less refreshing. In Silicon Valley, it seems, there is no such thing as negative experience.

In an industry where, at least when you are funded by venture capital, you live, die, and are reborn by the J curve, failure is indeed the norm. But if both the high frequency and ultimate irrelevance of failure are inherent in the way money behaves in Silicon Valley, comfort with this idea seems to have received an additional boost in the twenty-first century: after the chastening of the dot-com bust, after the same press that had credulously accompanied tech's seemingly irresistible rise suddenly spun equally credulous tales of its decline, the tech industry made failure front and center of its resurgence.

In 2008, Cassandra (Cass) Phillipps, who started out in theater and event planning, founded FailCon. She came up with the event while working at a startup that was on the glide path to failure, frustrated that there wasn't a way to talk about what was happening to her and her coworkers. FailCon was born as a place to do just that. It was and was not strange in its timing: in 2008, failure was everywhere: mortgages and loans failed, then the companies extending those mortgages and loans, then the companies insuring those mortgages and loans; "too big to fail" was in every newscast. But failure didn't have this kind of ubiquity in Silicon Valley, and when it did occur, the panicked capital pouring in from all around the globe was there to soften the blow and let you try again.

Still, as Phillipps found, her event hit a nerve: Yes, there was hate mail, accusing her of damaging the industry's recently reacquired shine. But, she says today, there was "something in the zeitgeist that made storytelling about failure important and attractive." Tech was in the middle of a big boom; Silicon Valley seemed like the one outlier in an all-encompassing economic crisis, and yet there was finally a readiness to "start talking about how hard this is." FailCon was only one such event. There was also FailFair. There were the Fuckup Nights, which were basically open mics about failure.

Perhaps no cliché encapsulates this particular relationship to failure better than the ubiquitous mantra to "fail better" next time. Even by the standards of the concepts, ideas, and buzzwords explored in the preceding chapters, the route "fail better" has taken into d.school seminars and all-hands meetings is vertiginous. It is also immensely instructive. It will not surprise you to learn that the way "fail better" is commonly used misunderstands its source material. But the way it misunderstands its source material, and the ways in which that source material seems to offer itself up for misunderstanding in just the way Silicon Valley chooses to interpret it, makes it an appropriate final look at what tech calls thinking.

The phrase "fail better" comes from one of the more recent texts I consider in this book. Samuel Beckett (1906–1989), the last great Irish modernist, wrote "Worstward Ho," one of his final novellas, in 1983. The title is a play on "Westward ho!," an old phrase that was used as the title of an 1855 novel about a New World expedition, and that came to stand for the European spirit of expansion. "Worstward Ho" is a parody of this spirit. Like most of Beckett's work, it's a meditation on misunderstanding, failure, resignation. The prose has a cadence that lulls you in. Where the phrase "Westward ho!" projects into the distance, Beckett's phrases tend to surge forward only to get pulled back, like waves crashing on the shore. You can hear it when you read the piece out loud: "Ever tried. Ever failed. No matter. Try again. Fail again. Fail better."

When you remove "fail better" from this context, the first thing it loses is its rhythmic frame. "Fail better" is meant to resonate with the many other curt phrases that make up the passage, which together create a kind of vibration in Beckett's text. This vibration, rather than any plot ("Worstward Ho" doesn't seem to have one), the way these phrases respond to one another, creates the text's main through line. There is an important thematic element to the original context of "fail better" as well: the singsongy cadence of Beckett's prose makes it clear that failing better isn't supposed to usher one on to eventual success. Ever trying and ever failing are all there is. In fact, the entire text is about the way in which failure leads not to eventual salvation but inescapably toward frustration. (The narrative, such as it is, of "Worstward Ho" concerns a visit to a graveyard.)

Does the quote's provenance matter? In the context of an investigation into what tech calls thinking, yes. Firstly, because the way it is quoted is deeply revealing of how Silicon Valley quotes ideas in general. There's a whole register and context you have to un-hear in order to end up feeling cheered by "fail better." Secondly, the particular way in which Beckett's quote gets misappropriated suggests certain ideas he was very interested in and that the tech industry has trouble talking about. The very thing Beckett was after—failure as a condition of life, failure removed from the retrospective halo of eventual success—is something that the new tolerance for failure has, paradoxically enough, all but eradicated. By taking away failure's sting, the tech-mantra version of "fail better" has eliminated things only that particular sting could tell us.

Mark Zuckerberg may have encapsulated Silicon Valley's gospel of failure better than anyone in his address to the Harvard class of 2017: "J. K. Rowling got rejected twelve times before publishing *Harry Potter*. Even Beyoncé had to make hundreds of songs to get 'Halo.'" Those kinds of lists are everywhere in Silicon Valley, and they are perfectly meaningless. After all, the fact of rejection is no more a testament to the fact that one should keep going than it is to the fact that one should not.

The numbers cited are impressive only to people outside the fields these numbers come from. Anyone who's written a novel will tell you that just twelve rejections is a sign of some pretty smooth literary agenting. And writing a hundred songs to score a hit would likely be an excellent ratio for most people in the music industry. Narratives like this repackage the way trial and error already work across our culture into a kind of salvation narrative. Which ironically removes the "better" part from "fail better." Cass Phillipps found that as FailCon grew, "sharing your postmortems became cool," but "only really after you'd become successful some other way." There were lessons to be gleaned from the event, but those lessons became less and less about failure and more and more about success. The original vision that had made FailCon, and other events like it, so interesting was that it wanted to linger on how it feels to be in the middle of failure, on how to have an honest conversation about failure while one is failing or at least has not yet succeeded. But this was something FailCon wasn't able to provide.

Somewhat ironically, then, FailCon became a victim of its own success. In 2014, Phillipps canceled FailCon San Francisco, telling *The New York Times* that "it's in the lexicon that you're going to fail." An event that had been conceived as an antidote to hagiographic developers' conferences and tech booster-fests like TechCrunch Disrupt had become an extension of these events. It was emblematic of the way failure got co-opted by the top, by those eager to show that, yes, they too had some hard times, before they drive away to Atherton in their Model X. Open talk about failure had started out as an important corrective, but it had been swallowed by the system.

Around the time Phillipps decided to shutter FailCon SF, Elizabeth Holmes put up a Michael Jordan quote in the

Theranos headquarters in Palo Alto that said, "I've missed more than 9,000 shots in my career. I've lost almost 300 games. 26 times, I've been trusted to take the game winning shot and missed. I've failed over and over and over again in my life. And that is why I succeed." The company made a fetish of the failure discourse: its main product, the blood-testing machine called Edison, was named after a famous (and probably misattributed) quote from Thomas Alva Edison—"I have not failed 10,000 times. I have found 10,000 ways that won't work." As with almost any artifact associated with Theranos, this obsession with getting it wrong now seems almost cosmically ironic—not because Theranos ultimately failed, but because Theranos wasn't actually playing. What shots was Theranos even taking that it could have missed? What ways did it find that didn't work? Thanks to the startup's incredible secrecy and its legal war machine, we still don't know. Now it is up to the U.S. District Court in San Jose to figure it out.

One thing the misappropriation of Beckett's "fail better" has in common with the Jordan and Edison quotes is its mode of address: they are exhortations to self-optimize, addressed to a single individual. They seem out of place in the lobby of a large company and more appropriate in a freshman dorm room, where one single person can look up at them through tears of frustration from time to time. Silicon Valley founders, inventors, and moneymen routinely embrace the first-person plural when they're really talking about themselves—although they will frame it in such a way that you cannot quite tell whether they are using the royal "we" or imagine a phantom team around them at all times. They like, in other words, to leap between the individual and the team in a way that doesn't always feel legitimate—and failure may be one place where it really isn't.

This focus on the individual is significant. If these motivational quotes spin a salvation narrative, it is one of individual salvation. Philosophers still debate the idea that certain aspects of human existence are progressing toward greater refinement. But none of them think that our individual lives point in an upward trajectory. As a species, we may yet do things in the future that you and I cannot dream of today, but as individuals, the window of self-transcendence closes pretty much when we leave high school. If anything, societal progress tends to evacuate our individual failures of meaning. Think of the last generation of people to die of a disease before it is eliminated. Think of the last woman burned as a witch before people wised up. The bromides about Michael Jordan and J. K. Rowling are premised on the idea that we're all Michael Jordan and J. K. Rowling.

That wouldn't have to be the intent of the posters. In 1818, the German philosopher G.W.F. Hegel said that "in contemplating history," which he called "the slaughterbench at which the happiness of peoples, the wisdom of states, and the virtue of individuals have been sacrificed," a question forces itself upon us: "To what principle, to what final purpose, have these monstrous sacrifices been offered?" Could all the failures and colossal wrecks have been worth it, to serve some overarching purpose? It's a common, compelling, and often highly controversial idea in the history of philosophy. But it's very much not the idea behind "fail better." Even if they didn't insist that you—yes, you—could one day write "Halo," the motivational bromides would have to spell out what end our enormous sacrifices serve. That is called utopianism, and for all of tech's obsession with the future, it is something the industry is uncomfortable with. Because utopianism is political: it spells out what will exist and what won't exist in the good, true, and just state to come. Tech is fond of the weak utopianism of its bottom line—getting everyone into a self-driving car, say, or getting a human on Mars, or getting you a burrito in under thirty minutes.

If Silicon Valley has domesticated failure, it has done so as part of a self-help ethos. It is interested in the way failure can make a better you, and the language it borrows frames failure as a route to an eventual redemption. The design-thinking process taught by the Stanford d.school has five steps: Empathize, Define, Ideate, Prototype, and Test. It's in step four, Prototype, that failure becomes most important: you need to "fail fast" and "iterate quickly." You're done with empathy and ideation; it's now about your own expectations for yourself. The most popular class that teaches this method has very little to do with gadgets or websites. It is called Designing Your Life, and is taught by Dave Evans and Bill Burnett. The class, and the successful 2016 book, *Designing Your Life: How to Build a Well-Lived, Joyful Life,* that Evans and Burnett spun off from it, are premised on the idea that, as Burnett put it in a TEDx Talk, "the most interesting design problem is your life."

Significantly, d.life, as the class is known, returns design thinking to a sphere that very clearly inspired a lot of its ideas in the first place, but which the field often hid under a lot of jargon. Much of this stuff, it turns out, has been about self-help all along—with particular emphasis on the *self* part. For all the talk about empathy (which is, after all, the first step of design thinking), the focus is usually on the creative self: in practice, the Empathize step consists of some pretty minimal observation of other people in action and maybe filming them interacting with an object or a space. It could uncharitably be described as an unempathetic person's idea of empathy.

Sociology has long regarded the self-help phenomenon as responding to a particularly modern, and particularly capitalist, kind of loneliness. From Dale Carnegie's advice for the lone salesman to Spencer Johnson's *Who Moved My Cheese?* (1998), self-help literature offered to give shape to lives that had lost an earlier sense of orientation and embedding; lives whose coordinates and fixed points once felt objectively valid, but now felt worryingly up for grabs. The more we are detached from communal standards and an in-group whose views validate us, the more we are alone with ourselves and the cold, unflinching gaze of society—and we have to seek validation via what we consume, how we decorate our homes, how we take care of ourselves, and so forth. Self-help is frequently about asserting our autonomy, not by rejecting societal norms or our historical situation but by understanding them better than other individuals in society, and thereby coming out ahead of others in our situation.

But d.life is perhaps less interesting as a self-help project than as a set of discursive tricks used to elide that fact. Like much of self-help, it borrows from pop psychology. More specifically, a lot of its central operations are borrowed from cognitive behavioral therapy. As the historian Lee Vinsel has pointed out, the concept of "reframing" is basically a direct carryover from the idea common in CBT that we need to challenge "negative thought patterns." We may inhabit a distorted version of the world around us, and our coping mechanisms may turn against us; CBT promises to reframe our relationships and the habits by which we manage those relationships.

At least part of the reason CBT has become so influential is that it gets at some pretty old ideas about human nature. There is a pronounced stoicism to it, but also a very American work ethic: with a can-do spirit, you can make the necessary adjustments to your perception of yourself and your environment. More important, however, CBT combines these very old ideas with some far more recent intuitions: the idea that people can be programmed and, more significantly, reprogrammed. Design thinking in some way retranslates this kind of thinking into the technological sphere from which it originated. Or, put another way, in design thinking, self-improvement and programming become one.

But if these ideas come from CBT, the vocabulary used to describe them seems to come from somewhat less mainstream fields. The term "reframing," for instance, comes out of something called neuro-linguistic programming. The idea of a cybernetic psychology took off after World War II, as cybernetics and information theory began to reshape many disciplines. In the 1970s, several of Gregory Bateson's students pioneered the field of neuro-linguistic programming. Associated above all with Richard Bandler and John Grinder, neuro-linguistic programming remains influential today, even though it is widely regarded as a pseudoscience. Although NLP practitioners resist codifying their teaching, the basic idea is that we can reprogram behavioral patterns by changing our mental processes and the language we use in reflecting on them. They mean the "programming" quite literally, declaring that in communication there are no mistakes—everything is feedback.

The focus on failure is a central node along which, it seems, Silicon Valley translates computational concepts into psychological theories—or, as critics would have it, self-help platitudes. Mythologizing failure magically turns empathy into looking at yourself. Hearing "fail better" out of context, it turns out, allows you to reframe your navel-gazing as a posture of humility.

⁘

To Mark Zuckerberg's credit, his 2017 Harvard graduation speech actually acknowledged the biggest problem with the gospel of failure: that its proper functioning presumes (and depends on) a thoroughly middle-class, young, white, and abled subject. "The greatest successes come from having the freedom to fail," he said, and added a little later, "I know lots of people who haven't pursued dreams because they didn't have a cushion to fall back on if they failed."

Zuckerberg is right: in capitalism in the United States at large, but most egregiously where the tech industry is concerned, the meaning of failure depends on who is doing the failing. For tech, failure is always assumed to be temporary; for everyone else, it's terminal. Taxi-cab companies are going out of business because they're losing money? Creative destruction, my friend—sink or swim. Uber hemorrhages cash? Well, that's just a sign of how visionary the company is. This double standard justifies the exploitation of workers outside of the tech industry—and, in certain cases, the exploitation of workers within it. After all, in a world in which all failure is assumed to be temporary, there are recourses that workers at startups do not avail themselves of. Rather than sue the company that promised them options it never delivered, then went out of business and left them broke, they will quietly move on to the next startup, try harder, fail better. The tech industry is good at getting even its most well-compensated employees to forget one simple fact: whatever else failure is about, it is also about responsibility, particularly for one another.

And the question of whether or not someone gets to "fail fast" and then "iterate" is deeply dependent on social factors. Race and class are two of them, but the simplest is probably age. In 2017, after a string of terrible publicity, Uber's then CEO, Travis Kalanick, admitted, "I must fundamentally change as a leader and grow up." Even in a place as chockablock with balding skateboarders and middle-aged trick-or-treaters as San Francisco, a forty-year-old CEO of a seventy-billion-dollar company casting himself as an overenthusiastic kid who just needs to get his shit together was seen as a bit much. Not everyone can be or act young. And in the Valley, for most people, both have become unsustainable.

Failing in Silicon Valley is often a prerogative of the young—or, in Kalanick's case, the young-acting. The speakers and attendees of FailCon, for instance, "totally clustered," Cass Phillipps notes. They ranged in age from twenty-eight to forty-five. The speakers were usually talking about failures that were a few years in the past—with the notable exception of one unfortunate presenter who had to change his topic three weeks before the event because his next venture failed. Founders and investors sometimes talk about a "runway": failure doesn't matter because you still have a lot of time to achieve liftoff.

This runway gives failure a local component. In Silicon Valley, failure comes encased in bubble wrap, precisely because the people who gave the money and the people who blew it on a terrible idea are likely to work together again, or at least run into each other at parties. But what about those who aren't? If you are not in their circle, then an altogether different set of rules applies. Many of the employees who have forgone sleep, pay, health care, and a social life for the benefit of now-worthless shares will not be instrumental in making the next spin of the wheel the winning one.

There are many ways to close up shop in Silicon Valley: get acquired or acqui-hired, wind the company down, buy out your investors, or start anew as a small business. Depending on how a company dies, however, most of the employees will not be part of these transactions. Google won't acqui-hire the receptionist, or even the publicity person. Given the gender dynamics of Silicon Valley, this means that men usually are the ones who actually get to fail better. Given that many founders meet in college, it means that having gone to school with the top team is a plus. Those excluded are people who are treated as contractors and receive only equity, people who vest and then leave, people who are thrown out before they reach a vesting cliff after a mysteriously negative performance review.

And for these people, the law of repeat business reveals its ugly side. "None of this litigation happens in this industry, because nobody wants to be blackballed," a Silicon Valley lawyer once told me. Or, as an angel investor puts it, it's important that even a failed venture "facilitates the founder's story." Something similar seems to be true for employees: "I learned a lot" is what whoever is hiring, seeding, funding, or advising you on your next undertaking is going to want to hear. "The bastards screwed me out of a bunch of money" isn't.

Although it certainly isn't the most serious social problem with Silicon Valley's approach to failure, there is something deeply corrosive about the primacy of the story. The fetishizing of narratives of failure and one's eventual salvation from failure prevents what Cass Phillipps had in mind: to linger with failure, to make sense of it. Even if we could get to the utopia Zuckerberg seemed to be envisioning when he spoke at Harvard—one where everyone has the freedom to fail and society does its best to shield them from the most extreme consequences and to help them try again—there would be something troubling about the smoothness of such a system. After all, the gospel of failure assumes that all failure is just a stepping-stone to a greater success.

A lot of the younger venture capitalists are themselves highly successful founders, and the contingency of their own success hasn't yet sunk in. I've seen that people who strike it rich in Silicon Valley are generally dumbstruck by their own success. It comes so early, so unpredictably, so noiselessly—a bolt of lightning out of a blue sky. But people have to make sense of what happens to them. Some withdraw almost shyly from their own good fortune. But those who don't withdraw have to tell themselves stories about it. Why do they deserve their good fortune? What does it mean?

In his *Histories*, Herodotus tells the story of Polycrates, the tyrant of Samos in the sixth century B.C. Polycrates had succeeded in all of his endeavors—"no matter where he directed his campaigns, fortune consistently favored him." An allied ruler pointed out to him that there was such a thing as too much good fortune, and that, in order to ward off the jealousy of the gods, he ought to rid himself of something he valued above all. "Better to go through life experiencing bad as well as good luck than to know nothing but success." Polycrates decided to throw a priceless ring into the Aegean. But soon afterward, one of Polycrates's cooks brought him a most unexpected find: while preparing a fish for a feast at the palace, the kitchen staff had discovered their ruler's ring, and naturally returned it to him immediately. In terror, the allied ruler abandoned Polycrates, terrified by the extent and the relentlessness of Polycrates's good fortune.

The concepts explored in *What Tech Calls Thinking* can be read as so many attempts to grapple with something that resembles the strange fate of Polycrates—to find reasons why success has happened to certain individuals, certain companies, certain sectors of the economy, with such relentless force. But rather than casting away a precious ring, the kind of thinking I have traced in this book seeks to reframe itself to avoid Polycrates's dilemma.

Confronted with the uncanny smoothness of their ascent, Silicon Valley's protagonists fetishize the supposed break and existential risk entailed in dropping out of college to found a company. Confronted with the fact that the platforms that are making them rich are keeping others poor, they come up with stories to explain why this must necessarily be so. And by degrading failure, anguish, and discomfort to mere stepping-stones, they erase the fact that for so many of us, these stones don't lead anywhere.

The domestication of failure is where one generation of Polycrateses pass both their existential dilemma and their unwillingness to grapple with it on to the next. Because only those who have encountered the most stupefying, most inexplicable success will end up funding the next generation of startups. If you wind down, get acqui-hired, or make some other type of "graceful exit," you usually don't have the cash to do venture capital investing. Among those who do have that kind of cash, their sense of reality can be deeply warped—and maybe it has to be, as they are all a little shell-shocked by their extraordinary good fortune. Perhaps the most important thing Silicon Valley could still learn about failure is that it is powerless before its own success.

Acknowledgments

This book has been a long time coming as I, a humanist with very little experience in tech, started to get my bearings in the strange land of Silicon Valley. I'd like to thank the many folks who have spoken candidly with me over the years about the ideas they encounter in the tech industry. Some of the critiques rehearsed here were first inspired by these friends—and for that reason alone I probably shouldn't name them. I want to thank my editors at the *Frankfurter Allgemeine Zeitung*, the *Neue Zürcher Zeitung,* and *Zeit Online* for giving me one fascinating assignment around the Valley after another—sending me to Cougar Night at the Rosewood Sand Hill, asking me to do a deep dive into the R. Buckminster Fuller Collection at Stanford, and not giving out my email when a bunch of Elon Musk fans got mad at me.

The editors of *Logic*—Moira Weigel, Ben Tarnoff, Christa Hartsock, and Jim Fingal—were instrumental in making this book happen. So were several of the writers of that wonderful publication—Xiaowei Wang, Wendy Liu, and many others. My colleagues at Stanford, including Fred Turner, Jennifer Burns, Annika Butler-Wall, Persis Drell, Joshua Landy, and Denise Winters, helped me tell the Stanford part of the story as best I could. A massive thank-you to Ashe Huang, who fact-checked the Stanford portions of the book, and to Will Tavlin, who fact-checked all of it again. And an even bigger thank-you to Jackson Howard and Emily Bell at FSG, who helped hone this manuscript over many months.

I am indebted to the many scholars, essayists, and journalists whose work I draw on in *What Tech Calls Thinking*. For a full list of the sources I've referenced, visit adriandaub.com/#what-tech.